The western parts of the church at Neath

ABBEYS, PRIORIES AND
CATHEDRALS OF WALES

Mike Salter

FOLLY PUBLICATIONS

ACKNOWLEDGEMENTS

The plans were drawn by the author and are largely based on survey material obtained during field trips in Wales between 1970 and 2011. Plans of all six cathedrals and the abbeys of the Cistercians, Premonstratensians and Tironensians are given at 1:800, whilst the plans of the many Benedictine priory churches still in use are at 1:400. This should allow comparisons with similar buildings in other books in this series. The map was also prepared by the author.

Many thanks to Bernard Mutton, who appeared out of the blue just at the right moment with a collection of excavation reports needed by the author. The pictures of Cymer, Llanthony, Neath reredorter, Strata Florida tiled floor, Talley, the drawing of the capital from Strata Marcella, and material upon which the Carmarthen friary plan is based were all provided by him.

Thanks to Kate Miles for the pictures of Bardsey, Llangennith, and Pill.

All other photos were either taken by the author (the majority are recent digital pictures taken 2006 - 2010) or are old pictures from the author's collections.

Thanks also to Paul and Allan at Aspect Design for help with the cover design and other artwork matters.

Thanks also to Jude Bloomfield for doing some proof-reading.

AUTHOR'S NOTES

The aim of this book is to present information about, and comparative plans of, four dozen abbeys, priories, friaries and cathedrals in Wales dating between the early 12th century and the 1530s, when all the monastic houses were suppressed. Lack of space has prohibited much discussion of the post-monastic history of the sites. Detailed descriptions of modern furnishings, stained glass and monuments in those buildings remaining at least partly in use also lie outside the intended scope of the book. This book particularly focuses on some lesser known buildings such as the priories of Caldey and Monkton, and also the ten Welsh friaries, which have not been much featured in other books, mainly because of the lack of accessible remains.

ABOUT THE AUTHOR

Mike Salter is 58 and has been a professional writer and publisher since he went on the Government Enterprise Allowance Scheme for unemployed people in 1988. He is particularly interested in the planning and layout of medieval buildings and has a huge collection of plans of churches and castles he has measured during tours (mostly by bicycle, motorcycle or on foot) throughout all parts of the British Isles since 1968. Wolverhampton born and bred, Mike now lives in an old cottage beside the Malvern Hills. His other interests include walking, maps, railways, board games, all kinds of morris dancing, mumming, playing percussion instruments and calling folk dances.

Ewenny Priory

CONTENTS

A map of the sites appears inside the front cover

GENERAL INTRODUCTION

Little is known for certain of the origins of Christianity in Wales and there is much uncertainty as to how it developed and was organised before the 11th century. By the mid 6th century St David was the head a monastery at the place that bears his name, and St Deiniol had been installed as bishop of Bangor. At about the same time St Cadfan was head of a monastery at Tywyn and St Seiriol ruled at Penmon. By the 7th century there were other monasteries at Clynnog Fawr, Llanbadarn Fawr and Llandeilo. The abbots of these monasteries seem to have also been styled as bishops.

The Celtic monasteries did not adopt the code or Rule of St Benedict written c529, which, with modifications and changes of emphasis by the different orders, became the basis of all monastic life in mainland Europe throughout the medieval period. The Celtic monasteries remained quite independent of each other. They sent out missionaries but failed to establish and maintain a proper system of parochial churches tended by local priests overseen by a bishop who assumed spiritual authority over an area known as a diocese. The word cathedral was used to describe a principal church in a diocese in which a bishop had his seat or throne, known as a cathedra. Having discarded bishops in favour of abbots an eventual decline of the Celtic church in the face of competition by the highly organised Roman church was inevitable.

England had many Benedictine abbeys established during the Saxon period and an even larger number of small priories established by the Normans after they arrived there in the late 11th century. In South Wales in the early 12th century the new Norman lords established priories of Benedictine monks not far from the castles forming their main seats at Abergavenny, Brecon. Cardiff, Cardigan, Chepstow, Kidwelly, and Monmouth, whilst Monkton lies opposite Pembroke, Ewenny is only three miles upstream from Ogmore, and Usk had a Benedictine nunnery. The vanished priory of Goldcliff was unusual in not being associated with a nearby castle. Benedictine monks were also introduced to replace Celtic priests at Llangennith on Gower. The priories served as lordly burial places and as power-houses of prayer aimed at redeeming the souls of patrons who were all warriors guilty of committing a variety of sins, particularly having broken the commandment about not killing other men. The monasteries also usually provided guest accommodation for travellers and some medical and clerical services. The mother houses of the priories lay either in England or France. Some of these priories, especially Kidwelly, Llangennith and Monkton, often had less than the normally accepted minimum of a prior and twelve monks, although monks from the mother houses were often sent over to recuperate from illness or conduct special business.

The Normans also established four dioceses in Wales, each with a new cathedral served by secular clergy replacing Celtic priests. All four belonged to the province of Canterbury. The diocese of St Davids served Deheubarth, roughly corresponding to the later counties of Pembroke, Cardigan and Carmarthen. In SE Wales the diocese of Llandaff composed several marcher lordships later re-organised as the counties of Brecon, Glamorgan, Monmouth and Radnor. The diocese of Bangor served the principality of Gwynedd. However the eastern part of what later became the county of Merioneth was in the 12th century claimed by the princes of Powys and became part of the diocese of St Asaph later corresponding to the counties of Denbigh, Flint and Montgomery. This arrangement of diocesan boundaries in Wales survived unchanged until in the 1920s the industrialised and heavily populated diocese of Llandaff was divided in three. Monmouthshire became a see with a cathedral created out of the parish church at Newport, and Brecon priory became a cathedral serving a see of Brecon and Swansea comprising the counties of Brecon, Radnor and western Glamorgan.

The last scanty remains of the Cistercian abbey of Cwm Hir

The earliest order of reformed Benedictines adhering to a stricter interpretation of the Rule were the Cluniacs. In Wales they had a small priory at St Clears. Another order of reformed Benedictines, the Tironensians, noted for encouraging craftsmen to join them, had an abbey at St Dogmaels and small dependent priories at Caldey and Pill. Two other reformed Benedictine orders, the Carthusians and the Valliscaulians, had no houses in Wales, but by the 13th century another reformed Benedictine order, the Cistercians, had become the most numerous order of monks in Wales, with abbeys at Aberconwy, Basingwerk, Cwm Hir, Cymer, Llantarnam, Margam, Neath, Strata Marcella, Strata Florida, Tintern, Valle Crucis and Whitland. The abbeys at Basingwerk and Neath originally belonged to the order of Savigny which merged with the Cistercians in 1147. Several of these abbeys had Welsh princes rather than Norman lords as patrons. Whereas the Benedictines had an emphasis on liturgy, the Cistercians favoured simplicity, remoteness and self-sufficiency. Their churches never formed part of the parochial system. The Cistercians liked remote valleys where their lay brethren (who spent considerably less time in church than the choir-monks) could tame wilderness and turn formerly harsh environments into highly organised and eventually profitable farms raising crops and huge flocks of sheep.

All Cistercian houses ranked as abbeys regardless of their size and importance, and were ruled by an abbot with a prior as his deputy, and large establishments would also have a sub-prior as third in command. Houses of the other orders were generally smaller and most of them ranked as priories with a prior as the head (or prioress in a nunnery). There was no fixed rule about the ranking of a monastery as an abbey or priory. Some abbeys were small and poor. Outside of Wales some of the priories were large and wealthy.

The church of the old priory on Caldey Island

The nave of Llanthony Priory

In addition to the various orders of monks there were two orders of canons regular, so called to distinguish them from the lay clergy that served the four cathedrals and the parish churches. Regular canons also lived a cloistered life as part of a community, sleeping in dormitories and eating in refectories and adhering to the basic monastic vows of poverty, chastity and obedience. However they also went out into the wider community to preach and take services in the parish churches under their control. The western part or nave of their own abbey or priory church usually served the needs of a parish. In South Wales they had just three priories, Carmarthen and Haverford-west, being new Norman foundations each associated with a castle and walled town, whilst Llanthony was more remotely located and probably on the site of a former celtic monastery. In North Wales Celtic monasteries at Bardsey, Beddgelert, and Penmon all became small Augustinian priories during the early 13th century. The more rather austere Premonstratensians or white canons also used the rule of St Augustine. Their only Welsh house was at Talley, built under patronage of the Welsh princes of Deheubarth.

Details of the Chancel arch at St Clears

There were also two military orders of knights who lived as monks. The Knights Templar had no major establishments in Wales, but the Knights Hospitaller, who used the Rule of St Augustine, had a commandery at Slebech in the vulnerable northern part of the Norman lands in Pembrokeshire and another at Ysbyty Yfan in North Wales. Few knights ever lived in them and most of the inhabitants at the commanderies would have been servants and lay officials.

Wales also had ten houses representing four different orders of friars. These establishments have been largely overlooked until fairly recently because little remains of most of them and historical information about them is scanty. All the Welsh friars were mendicants and were not supposed to hold property apart from the land on which their house, cemetery, gardens and water supply were located. Sometimes the communities even had to pay rents on parts of these and it was generally accepted that friars continually had to beg for alms as well as preach. Thus mendicant friars usually had to rely on the continued generosity of local benefactors both for building works and everyday subsistence. Consequently friars' houses were generally within towns large enough to be able to support such communities of beggars. The friars provided a supply of extra preachers and they were often well supported by royalty and bishops, although as competitors for local charity they were generally unpopular with the established communities of monks and regular canons and also with the local parochial clergy. The Dominicans had houses in Brecon, Cardiff and Haverfordwest by the 1240s. Franciscans arrived at Llanfaes in 1237 and by the late 13th century they also had houses at Cardiff and Carmarthen, whilst the Carmelites had a house at Denbigh. The Augustinian friary at Newport founded in 1377 was the last medieval religious house to be established within Wales

Arches in the north transept east wall at St Davids

A large monastery could have quite a number of officials under the abbot and prior. Church services were organised and managed by the precentor, who was the chief singer and also the librarian and archivist. He might have an assistant known as the succentor, The sacrist looked after the fabric of the church and its ornaments, vestments and furnishings, usually having an office beside or near the east end of the church. His deputy the sub-sacrist rang the bells to summon the brethren to services. The cellarer was in charge of supplies of food and drink, often extending to dominion over the mills, brew-house and agricultural work at the abbey's possessions, although these might be looked after by a lay steward, whilst the sub-cellarer or kitchener had responsibility for the preparation and cooking of food. The fraterer was in charge of serving the food and drink and the cleaning of the refectory and the lavatory outside it where the monks washed their hands before eating. A chamberlain was in charge of providing bedding, hot water for shaving and occasional baths, and the provision of clothing for the brethren. Novice monks usually used some of the lower rooms in the east range and were under the supervision of the novice master. Sick and elderly monks went to an infirmary separate from the main buildings (usually further east). It was looked after by the infirmarer and was initially the only place where meat other than fish was served. Monks regularly went there to be bled (which was thought to be good for the health) and were allowed to eat meat to help recover afterwards. Most monasteries had a guest house as from a patron's point of view that was an important function of them, and it required another official to administer it. In the larger monasteries guest houses were mansions of some size suitable for visitors of high rank with their retinues. Idle conversation was discouraged by monastic rules but of course officials would have needed to have spoken frequently to each other and to other monks and servants under their control.

The rule of St Benedict allowed for a daily monastic routine with up to seven services, with some variance according to the season of the year and certain feast days requiring special services, extra masses or processions. Some of the office holders must have been excused from attending services at certain times in order to carry out their duties. In some communities menial tasks such as cooking and washing were done by servants. The day started with Matins in the middle of the night, which was quickly followed by Lauds. Then the monks were allowed the second part of their sleep for about four hours before returning to church for the service of Prime. Some reading time followed, then the all-important masses for the souls of benefactors and their families and then some refreshment was allowed before the Lady Mass. Afterwards the monks gathered in the chapter house to hear read to them a portion of the rule under which they lived. Weekly duties were then allocated, faults were corrected and any business conducted relating to such matters as administration of estates, construction or repair of buildings, appointment of officers or the admission of novices. The next service, Tierce or High Mass might be followed by a procession around the church and cloister. The monks then took their main meal of the day in the refectory. A good choice of foodstuffs might usually be on offer. Originally meat was served only to sick and elderly monks in the infirmary but later on meat eating became normal. Monks were not allowed to indulge in idle chat during meals and were obliged to listen to one of their number reading religious tracts from a pulpit in the refectory. Afternoons were used for study, writing, the teaching of novices, short periods of recreation, or just a nap during the longer days of summer. A second meal was taken after Vespers or Evensong and after Compline the monks would retire to bed for three hours or so for the first part of their sleep until wakened again for Matins.

By the late medieval period many of the monasteries were not in a healthy state. Numbers of monks, canons and friars were down, and standards had become lax in some houses. Some of the smaller houses were suppressed in 1535-6 and by early 1538 all the others had closed and their inmates dispersed. Some got pensions and others became Anglican clergy but many were left to fend for themselves. Usually the monastic lands were soon sold off to local gentry. Before long very little remained of the friaries in the towns, where there was pressure for rapid redevelopment. The only standing remains are of the churches at Brecon and Denbigh. The houses of Augustinian and Premonstratensian canons and Cistercian monks also soon became ruinous. At Neath, Margam and Vale Crucis parts of abbeys were incorporated in later mansions. Cistercian sites were less prone to redevelopment, and quite a lot still remains both of churches and of the domestic buildings, with quite impressive ruins remaining at Basingwerk, Neath, Tintern and Vale Crucis, and more minor remains at Cwm Hir, Cymer, Talley, and Whitland, whilst Aberconwy and Margam are rare instances of the naves of former Cistercian churches later being used as parts of parish churches.

Hardly anything remains of the cloisters and domestic buildings of the Benedictine priories, but the naves of their churches often served parishioners and remained in use. Almost complete churches have survived at Abergavenny, Brecon, Ewenny, Kidwelly, Llangenneth, and Monkton. The churches at Cardigan and Monmouth have been much rebuilt and only the naves now remain at Chepstow and Usk. Of houses of reformed Benedictines other than Cistercians there remains a modest church at St Clears, a small but almost complete layout of roofed buildings at Caldey, and considerable ruins at St Dogmaels. Other relics include a ruined church of the Knights Hospitaller at Slebbech. The four cathedrals all still survive despite attempts in the 16th century to replace St Davids with a new cathedral at Carmarthen and St Asaph with a new cathedral within the town walls at Denbigh. All four cathedrals were in a semi-ruinous state before a series of 19th and 20th century restorations.

The chapter house at Margam

ARCHITECTURAL INTRODUCTION

Little remains of the pre-12th century Celtic monasteries but excavations have revealed footings of the monastery on Burry Holm, and there are fragments of crosses and funerary monuments of various kinds. Relics of the last few generations of these communities are the towers with pyramidal stone roofs at neighbouring Priestholm and Penmon, with other parts of a cruciform church at the latter. The original churches seem to have been simple in form, consisting of a nave for the congregation and a shorter, narrower and lower chancel to contain the altar and its attendant priests.

The earliest Norman bishops of the four sees each began construction of a new cathedral in the early 12th century. Of these buildings there remain just the sanctuary arch at Llandaff and some walling in the choir south wall at Bangor. At St Davids the six bay aisled nave is good Late Norman work of the 1180s and 1190s with the round arch predominating, whilst the choir and transepts with pointed arches and narrower bays date from soon after 1200. This is the premier cathedral of Wales in every sense, being larger, more ornate, and less restored than other Welsh cathedrals, although it is smaller than most of the English medieval cathedrals. Llandaff has two fine western towers (one 15th century, the other 19th century) and a late 13th century Lady Chapel, but it lacks the transepts and central tower regarded as normal for European cathedrals. St Asaph has a 14th century aisled nave and Bangor has 16th century arcades. They have central towers, transepts and aisleless presbyteries, but despite their size (particularly their width) they have more the character of large parish churches.

It often took several generations to complete the construction of a cathedral or an abbey church. No abbot, prior, bishop or patron ever expected to live long enough to see a building that they had laid out and begun fully completed. Usually work started at the east end of the church and progressed westwards as far as the crossing in the hope of roofing those parts within twenty years or so. Then there would be often a lull whilst more materials and funds were accumulated before work could be resumed to complete the nave. By then the east end was often considered too small or old fashioned and needed to be remodelled or entirely rebuilt. This is what happened at St Davids Cathedral in the late 12th century.

Bangor Cathedral from the SE

The south side of Llandaff Cathedral, showing the chapter house

Monastic churches were usually cruciform with the four arms abutting a central tower, although towers were not common in the houses of the Cistercians, who regarded them as ostentatious. Another feature of Cistercian churches was the suppression or mini-malisation of the triforium gallery, which was mostly decorative rather than functional, dividing the clerestory windows from the arcades below. Cistercian abbey churches tended to have just a short presbytery east of a pair of transepts each with two or three eastern chapels. In Wales this layout is best preserved in the early 13th century church at Vale Crucis. Here the east wall has three lower lancets and two smaller upper ones piercing an upper widening of the pilaster buttresses between the lower windows.

The choir stalls of Cistercian monks usually lay within the eastern part of the nave, whilst the rest of the nave was allocated for use by lay brothers. This resulted in some extremely long aisled naves in their churches. There were only five bays at Vale Crucis, and six at Tintern, but Basingwerk, Neath, Strata Florida and Aberconwy as rebuilt at Maenan each had seven bays, Margam and Whitland had eight, whilst Strata Marcella had ten bays and Cwm Hir had as many as fourteen. At Cwm Hir and its daughter house at Cymer only a nave now survives and there is no certainty that a presbytery was ever begun. The late 12th century piers at Margam are rectangular in plan but piers with shafts facing the cardinal points and intermediate shafts were the norm by the 13th century. At Strata Florida piers of this type were set upon walls rather than rising from floor level. Five bays of arcading from Cwm Hir now reset in the parish church at Llanidloes have multiple shafts and moulded arches. The Premonstratensian abbey of Talley had a similarly long nave as planned, but only the eastern four of the eight bays were ever completed. Some Cistercian churches later gained aisled presbyteries, as at Margam c1220, at Neath and Tintern c1270-1330, where large new churches replaced much smaller ones with aisleless naves, and Aberconwy (at Maenan) of c1290-1320.

Late Norman south doorway at Llandaff

The infirmary at St Dogmaels

The naves of Benedictine and Augustinian priories were often used by parishioners. The 12th century nave at Chepstow and the 14th century nave at Brecon were fully aisled but the naves at Kidwelly and Monkton were aisleless. Kidwelly has a porch tower on the north side and Monkton has a south transeptal tower, whilst the priory at Llangennith has a north transeptal tower. Churches serving tiny priories without a full claustral layout often had a layout more normal for a purely parochial church, as at St Clears, which consists of a late medieval west tower, a nave and a narrower chancel, with a Norman arch between the latter two. The aisleless 13th century nave at Haverfordwest (which was not parochial) later gained a tower in a very unusual location over its eastern end, just west of the transepts. Some parochial naves of monastic churches had a single aisle on the side away from the cloister, as at Abergavenny, Ewenny and Usk. Both these latter two churches have 12th century central towers, and Ewenny retains a vaulted presbytery of the same period and a south transept with round arches towards a pair of eastern chapels. Low walls remain of the northern transept and its chapels. The Tironian church at St Dogmaels retains the base of a mid 12th century east apse projecting from the south transept. Originally the north transept had a similar apse and so did the presbytery until given a square-ended extension over a crypt in the 13th century. Brecon priory retains a still-roofed presbytery of c1200-07 with five lancet windows in the east wall and stepped groups of three in each bay in the side walls. Here the innermost of the pairs of chapels east of each transept were two bays long. The northern chapels were replaced by one larger single chapel in the 14th century. Llanthony was the only church in Wales to have a triple-towered arrangement with twin western towers in addition to a central tower, although this layout was common in England and it appears that this layout was originally intended at Talley.

Friars' churches usually had aisleless choirs, as in the 13th century examples still remaining at Brecon and Denbigh, the former still roofed. Transepts were common in late medieval friars' churches in Ireland but there is little evidence of them in England and Wales, where the norm was for a central walking space between the choir and nave with a narrow tower raised over it. No friary church towers now remain in Wales. Foundations of a fully aisled nave remain at the Dominican friary at Cardiff. The Dominican friary church at Brecon had a north aisle beside the nave and the Franciscan friary at Carmarthen is also known to have had a wide north aisle.

The vaulted chapter house at Valle Crucis Abbey

In most monasteries the cloister was located on the sunnier southern side of the church. Occasionally the necessities of water supply or drainage led to the cloister being on the north side, as at Tintern and the Dominican friary at Cardiff. The cloister of St Davids Cathedral is also placed on the north side. At Caldey, which is too small to have a cloister as such, the court enclosed by the domestic buildings also lies on the north side. Normally the east range would contain a communal dormitory on the upper floor with a latrine either on the east side or at the far end from the church. A stair from the cloister to the dormitory was used in the day-time but a stair in the adjoining transept allowed a more direct access into the church at night. Below would be the sacristy, the chapter house, a passage leading out to a cemetery further east, a warming room or calefactory containing the only fireplace in the main buildings, and rooms used for instructing novices. The chapter house often projected beyond the east range. Sometimes the range only contained an ante-room, with the chapter house itself entirely beyond the range, as at St Dogmaels following 14th century rebuilding, and as at Margam, which retains a fine 13th century chapter house which is circular internally but twelve-sided externally. The chapter house at Llanthony had an unusual polygonal east end. Vale Crucis has a well preserved late 14th century chapter house vaulted in three by three bays with four central piers. It was common for a chapter house to have a central entrance without a door and flanked on either side by a two-light window facing the cloister walk. Usually a stone bench ran all the way round the room providing seating.

The church at Tintern seen from across the infirmary cloister

The range opposite the church usually contained the refectory. This room normally had a projection in an outside wall to contain a pulpit from which one of the brethren would read to the others at meal-times. In Cistercian houses the refectory was a large room often projecting southwards from the cloister instead of parallel to it, as at Basingwerk, Neath, Tintern and Valle Crucis, each of which retain substantial remains of late 12th or 13th century claustral ranges. This layout allowed space for a kitchen adjoining the cloister to the west of the refectory. A lavatory or hand-washing recess was usually provided off the cloister near the refectory entrance, as at Neath. The west range might contain rooms for the use of guests or the abbot or prior over vaulted cellars or offices. In Cistercian houses this range was originally allocated for the use of lay brothers, with a second dormitory set over a second refectory. Very few western ranges of Cistercian houses in England and Wales survive as complete as that at Neath.

At Tintern the lower walls remain of a second cloister beyond the east range with beyond it an infirmary composed of two main ranges, one with a hall with side chambers and the other with several kitchens. Beyond the NE corner of the second cloister lay a range containing the abbot's hall over offices, east of which lay his private room. Other monasteries had infirmaries and abbot's lodgings in a similar position relative to the other buildings, but on a less generous scale. At Caldey the prior's room lies in the upper storey of a block forming a semi-defensible embattled tower. Buildings assumed to have been prior's lodgings also remain at Monkton and Monmouth. Originally the head of a monastery was supposed to sleep in a dormitory with the other monks, but the heads of large establishments became in effect great temporal lords and were either frequently away or kept busy conducting the business affairs of the house. By the 13th century the head of a monastery normally had his own suite of rooms.

The church and claustral buildings of a monastery usually lay within a precinct wall which also enclosed barns and other stores, workshops and offices which might be partly or wholly timber-framed and have thus rarely survived. Some of the English abbeys had huge crenellated gateways to their precincts. A modest gateway remains at Brecon and Ewenny has substantial remains of a semi-defensible precinct wall with two strong gatehouses and three other towers. The cathedral precinct at St Davids retains a ruinous surrounding wall. Of the four gateways the main one adjoins an octagonal bell-tower high above the cathedral itself. Little now remains of another substantial bell-tower also set high above the cathedral of Llandaff.

North gatehouse and precinct wall at Ewenny Priory

The ball-tower and main gateway to the precinct at St Davids

Piscinae and sedilia in the presbytery at Brecon

Of monasteries conforming to Rome in Wales Chepstow has the earliest work now remaining, with a nave of c1100-20. Ewenny has an almost complete church of the 1140s and 50s, and there are other 12th century remnants at Bangor, Llandaff, Newport, St Dogmaels, St Clears and Usk. A still-roofed nave of the 1180s remains at Margam and of about the same time is the nearly complete west range at Neath. The period 1190 to 1230 was particularly busy for building work, especially at the many Cistercian abbeys then newly founded. There is impressive work of that era in the naves of the cathedrals of St Davids and Llandaff and the latter also has a chapter house, the only one now surviving at a Welsh cathedral. Other major survivals include the presbytery of the Benedictine priory (now the cathedral) at Brecon, much of the Augustinian priory church of Llanthony, plus more minor or fragmentary work at several other places. Nearly all the monasteries had the majority of their claustral buildings erected or at least begun during this period, with fairly complete layouts preserved at the large abbeys of Neath and Tintern, and at the smaller abbeys of Basingwerk and Valle Crucis, all four of these being Cistercian.

Piers gradually assumed more complex shapes from the simple squares, rectangles and circles of the Norman period, with complex patterns of shafts, as at Llandaff and in the arcade from Cwm Hir now re-erected at Llanidloes parish church. Pointed arches became the norm after c1200, and the long narrow windows with pointed heads then common are called lancets. Triplets of lancets in gable walls remain at Aberconwy and Cymer and a particularly ornate set at St Davids. Before long lancets were placed close together and circles pierced between the heads as can be seen in windows in the fragments of the eastern parts at Margam. This led to the development of geometrical tracery best seen in the late 13th century church at Tintern. Neath has a large church of c1280-1330 but it is too ruined for much architectural detail to survive. Much of the churches at Abergavenny and Kidwelly are 14th century work, as are the west towers at Cymer and Monmouth, whilst the NW tower at Kidwelly is probably of c1400.

Llandaff Cathedral has an impressive NW tower of c1490, and the nave arcades and west tower at Bangor Cathedral are early 16th century, but surviving work of the 15th and early 16th centuries is not common amongst Welsh abbeys. The parochial north aisle at Usk has good 15th century work with two porches. At St Dogmaels the north transept was lengthened with diagonal corner buttresses and provision for a fan-vault, although the windows were of modest size. The west range at Caldey is probably 15th century. The Knights Hospitallers' church at Slebech has a north transept and porch tower of the early 16th century.

13th century windows at Margam Abbey

In the south wall of the eastern part of a church there would commonly be elaborate stone seats called sedilia for priests. Good examples of sets of three of them (the usual number) remain at Brecon and Kidwelly. Next to each altar would be a piscina for draining and washing out vessels used during a mass. Brecon Priory again has a set of three. Most of the stained glass windows, fonts, pulpits, screens and altars bore brightly painted images of saints and other icons which reformers associated with catholicism. Consequently hardly any of them survived the ravages of the 1530s and 40s. Fine painted tiles, however, remain at Bangor, Monmouth and Strata Florida and elsewhere, there are old screens at Brecon and Usk, and choir stalls with misericords at Abergavenny, St Asaph and St Davids. An unusual survival is a huge wooden figure at Abergavenny which formed the base of a tree of Jesse, a colossal structure once with many other figures. St Davids has a a fine bishop's throne and a huge pulpitum, both of them associated with Bishop Henry Gower, d1347.

The base figure of a former Tree of Jesse at Abergavenny

Originally the abbeys and cathedrals contained the majority of the medieval tombs with effigies in Wales since many of the ordinary parish churches were too small and humble to contain them. One of the main purposes of a monastery from a benefactor's point of view was to have a large and dignified place to house one's tomb, together with a body of priests available to take turns in saying masses at an adjacent altar for the good of your own soul and those of your friends, relatives and descendants. Large collections of effigies of 13th and 14th century ecclesiastics remain at the cathedrals of Llandaff and St Davids, along with the usual collections of effigies of knights with or without wives from the 14th century onwards. None of the Cistercian abbeys retains much in the way of monuments apart from fragments of cross-slabs, as at Valle Crucis, but empty tomb recesses survive in several places. Of the many priories of the Augustinians and Benedictines, Abergavenny has by far the best collection of monuments, with some splendid knights of the 14th, 15th and early 16th centuries. Brecon and Ewenny also retain some interesting monuments. Effigies were often painted, so that the shields of arms bore their real-life colours. Indents of brasses from the 14th century onwards also remain occasionally. Monuments frequently got moved around within churches. Some of those at Abergavenny have recently been moved in order to better display them. A number of tombs from friary churches, especially the Franciscan churches at Carmarthen and Llanfaes, were transferred to other churches at the suppression in order to ensure the survival of comparatively recently made effigies.

Tombs in the Herbert Chapel at Abergavenny

Tombs in the norch chair aisle at Llandaff

ACCESS TO THE MONUMENTS

Buildings still regularly used for services and normally open during daytime:
   The cathedrals of Bangor, Brecon, Llandaff, Newport, St Asaph, St Davids, and
   The former priory churches of Abergavenny, Cardigan, Chepstow, Ewenny,
   Kidwelly, Penmon, Usk and also the churches of Conwy (Aberconwy) and Ruthin
Cadw historic sites where entrance fees are payable: Neath, Tintern and Valle Crucis.
Exterior access: Beddgelert, Llangennith, Llanfair, Monmouth, St Clears.
Free access during daytime: Caldey, Cwm Hir, Cymer* Denbigh*, Haverfordwest,*
   Llanthony* St Dogmaels*, Talley*, Whitland   (*in custody of Cadw)
Ruins with free access within parks: Basingwerk, Cardiff and Margam

GAZETTEER OF ABBEYS, PRIORIES AND CATHEDRALS

ABERCONWY ABBEY   *Cistercian*   SH 781775   Replaced by town of Conwy

Monks sent out from Strata Florida in 1186 originally settled near Caernarfon but had transferred here by 1188, when their presence was noted by Gerald of Wales. Their patron was Llywelyn Fawr, and he and three of his family were buried within the church, which was damaged in 1245 by an English raid. In 1277 the abbey was the place where Llywelyn ap Gruffudd was forced to sign a treaty with Edward I of England. The church was damaged in the English invasion of 1283 and that same year the monks were transferred 12km southwards up the River Conwy to Maenan so that their church could become the parish church of St Mary of the walled town then being begun around it. The Englsh king allowed the monks some funds for rebuilding on the new site, east of the river, and the new church was on a larger scale, thus probably making a point about English superiority when it came to patronising monastic houses.

Conwy parish church is now mostly a 14th century building consisting of a west tower, north and south aisles with arcades of three bays, a south transept and a chancel as wide at the nave with a small chapel on the north side of it. The tower and the 17th century vestry north of it have been built against the original west wall of the nave and north aisle of the abbey. It has triple lancets over a fine doorway without fittings for a door which might be the chapter house entrance reset. Other possible remnants of the abbey church are the two tomb recesses in the south aisle and the lower parts of the east wall of the chancel, although its thickness is more typical for a parish church than a monastic one. The two 13th century windows in the chancel south wall must be reset as the original layout is likely to have had transepts slightly further east than the existing 14th century south transept. All but one bay of the original presbytery would have been flanked by the transept chapels. Other abbeys built under patronage of the princes of Gwynedd at Cwm Hir and Cymer had their naves built first (instead of the usual start at the east end) and the eastern parts of them were never completed, so it is possible that the same also happened at Aberconwy.

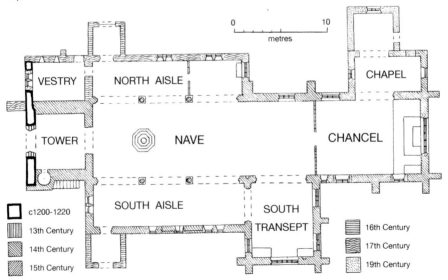

Plan showing remains of Aberconwy Abbey within Conwy parish church

The Maenan Abbey Hotel at SH 789657 stands on the site of the cloister of the new abbey, which appears to have had high quality buildings. South of the hotel lay the abbey church 65m long internally with the nave of seven bays and the presbytery of two wide bays and one short one both fully aisled. The crossing is now occupied by a cedar tree. Footings of the angle of the north transept and north aisle of the nave were found by excavation in 1924. The transepts were long enough for each have three chapels outside of the aisles. The church was irregularly laid out with the east end not a true right-angle and the north aisles of both parts much wider than the south aisles. Further west an early 15th century doorway is reset in a later wall. From the abbey have probably come a spiral stair in the upper part of an early 17th century tower at Bodysgallen and material in the mid 16th century west range at Gwydir Castle.

Remains of Aberconwy Abbey in Conwy parish church

Abergavenny priory church from the south

ABERGAVENNY PRIORY   *Benedictine*   SO 301141   On SE side of the town

The priory here was founded in the 1090s by Hamelin de Ballon as a cell of the abbey of St Vincent outside the city of Le Mans. The church was later rebuilt at the expense of John, Lord Hastings, who re-endowed the priory for a prior and twelve monks. Prior to an enquiry held by Adam, Bishop of Hereford in 1320 at the request of Lord Hastings the priory had become ruinous and was served only by five monks, who were said to be guilty of grave misdemeanours. From this time onwards the convent was more independent of the mother house and allowed to elect its own head. The priory was burned during the Glyndwr revolt of 1403, losing all its books and records. Several of the monks returned to Le Mans, and in 1411 the prior was given leave from Henry IV to ask for the mother house to send over three more monks to help celebrate masses in place of the secular chaplains which the convent had been forced to hire.

When the priory was suppressed it had a prior and four monks. Some of its revenues were applied to the founding of a new grammar school which took over the church of St John in the town. In return the townsfolk were allowed to take over for their services the whole of the priory church of St Mary. This ensured the survival of the magnificent Hastings and Herbert family tombs. The monuments are one of the finest collections in Wales and together with the choir stalls and Jesse Tree remnant are more important than the building itself, which is a very plain structure of red sandstone. The windows of the nave and wide north aisle and the five bay arcade between them are of 1881. The main object of interest in this part of the church is the Norman font bowl. The eastern parts are essentially all early 14th century, but the east windows of the presbytery and both chapels are 15th century or modern replacements and the north transept end window of five lights is of 1954. The central tower is narrower than the rather short transepts and is likely to perpetuate the original Norman plan form. The features are 14th century but some 12th century walling probably remains in the south transept. On each side of the choir is a two bay arcade with square piers into a chapel. Traces of a 15th century clerestory survive high up on the south side of the choir.

The Herbert Chapel at Abergavenny Priory, showing the many tombs

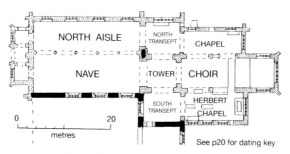

Plan of Abergavenny Priory Church

Font at Abergavenny Priory

The much altered east range of the claustral buildings also survives, with an east lancet at dormitory level, plus one original doorway. Other blocked windows and truncated chimney-breasts date from the late 16th or early 17th centuries.

A full set of canopied medieval stalls remains in the choir. The stall ends on the north side are poppy-heads. Those on the south side are carved as animals and here at one end the name Wynchester appears, commemorating a prior of 1493 to 1516. Several of the seats, however, appear to be a generation or two earlier. In the north transept lies a huge wooden reclining figure of Jesse which must have formed part of a huge 15th century reredos. The figure held the stem of a tree which once bore many other figures which still survived in a defaced condition in 1645. Also in the transept, but originally probably under a canopy in the north chapel, is a very fine wooden cross-legged effigy of John, second Lord Hastings, d1325. The effigy lies on a stone tomb chest made up of panels depicting knights, eight of them surviving of the original fourteen. In the north chapel lie a sandstone effigy of Eva de Braose, d1257, and a mid 14th century limestone effigy of a lady of the Hastings family with crimped hair who once held what is thought to have been a figure of a squirrel. There is also an effigy of Dr David Lewis, d1584, the first principal of Jesus College in Oxford.

The seven main monuments in the south chapel were all restored in the 1990s. The earliest are two from the same workshop and depict Sir Lawrence and Sir William de Hastings, who both died in 1348. Sir William lies against the south wall and has legs crossed at the ankles and feet resting on a greyhound. Sir Lawrence has his feet resting on a bull. His tomb has been moved southwards from its original location under the western arch of the chapel arcade. Centrally placed at the east end of the chapel is the superb alabaster tomb of Sir William ap Thomas, d1446 and his wife Gwladys, d1454. with twelve robed figures on each side, an unusual (in this context) representation of prophets and apostles. He is in full plate armour and she has a horned headdress with angels holding a cushion diamond-wise beneath her head. Under the eastern arch of the chapel arcade is another fine alabaster tomb with nine shield-bearing angels on the sides, the Virgin and Child flanked by St Margaret and St Catherine at the east end, and effigies on top of Sir Richard Herbert of Coldbrook, d1469, and his wife Margaret. At the east end of the south wall is a wall monument with an effigy of Richard Herbert of Ewyas, d1510. A panel on the backplate shows Richard and his wife with their six kneeling sons and two standing daughters below a scene of the Coronation of the Virgin. There are also defaced alabaster effigies of Andrew Powell, d1631, and his wife (now moved to the west end of the south wall) and of William Baker, d1648, and his wife near the west respond of the chapel arcade. Many old gravestones pave the floor.

BANGOR CATHEDRAL   *Secular Canons*   SH 581728   In middle of town

The original monastic enclosure of the time when St Deiniol became bishop of Gwynedd c546 lay to the east and below the cathedral and was sacked by sea-borne raid-
ers twice in the 7th century and again in 1073. The existing building was begun c1120
by Bishop David and was the burial place of Gruffudd ap Cynan, d1137, and his son
Owain Gwynedd, d1170. Of the Norman building there remains just the south wall of
its presbytery with a blocked round-arched window and a pilaster buttress marking the
start of the curvature of its east apse. Each transept also had an apsed east chapel.

The main apse was replaced by a longer east end begun c1220 under patronage
from Llywelyn Fawr. In the University Library lies the Pontifical of Anian, bishop here
from 1267 to 1307, under whom the south transept was rebuilt slightly longer. The
tomb recess there is thought to have been intended for an effigy of Ednyfed Fychan,
d1246. Bishop Anian II oversaw the same treatment of the north transept and the
replacement of the crossing arches after a fire in 1309. The roof and parapets of the
presbytery and the fine east window are of c1480-1500. The aisle windows appear to
be 14th century work but they could be reset and it is possible that the nave remained
aisle-less until the present arcades and clerestory were added by Bishop Skevington.
His arms appear on the stumpy west tower with diagonal buttresses added in 1532,
and the presbytery south window may also be of that date. The nave served as the
parish church of the mainly Welsh-speaking townsfolk. It was originally out of align-
ment with the eastern parts and an attempt to straighten it out has resulted in the west
tower being off-centre with it. Clearly the aisle walls with seven bays of openings were
built before the arcades of just six bays resulting in long responds at the ends.

The late medieval stained glass windows disappeared during a series of mid to late
18th century alterations and extensions. These were removed during a series of restorations begun in 1868 under George Gilbert Scott which saw the choir largely rebuilt
and the construction of the existing north vestries. Scott renewed the crossing arches
and the intention was to build a tall tower and spire over them until it became clear that
the foundations were inadequate to carry such a weight. The existing low tower there
is of 1966. The only ancient furnishings are one 15th century stall with a misericord,
some reset 14th century tiles with heraldry and birds probably made in Cheshire, and
a very rare 15th century wooden figure of Christ bound and crucified removed from the
church at Llanrwst but probably originally from the Dominican friary at Rhuddlan. The
only medieval effigy is a low-relief figure of a 14th century lady holding a rosary.

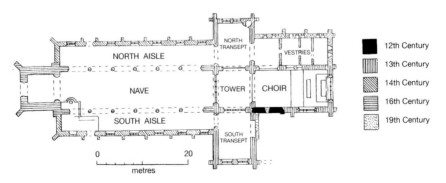

Plan of Bangor Cathedral

Bangor Cathedral from the SW

BANGOR FRIARY   *Dominican*   SH 583725   In middle of town

No traces now remain of the friary founded in 1251 by Geoffrey Glyn. Three cross-slabs now in the Bangor museum came from the original site near the shore at Hirael. The friary was damaged by Edward I's forces and later moved inland to a site now occupied by Bangor Grammar School.

BARDSEY ABBEY   *Augustinian*   SH 121221   On island at end of Lleyn peninsular

The only relic of the abbey of St Mary still in situ is a 13th century tower 5.6m square externally with its northern half still rising 8m high, now lying in the NW corner of a small graveyard. The lower stage has a doorway facing south, where there was clearly an adjoining structure, and a small window facing west. The tower may have formed a north transept, although there is no certainty that it actually formed part of a church. Bardsey was an ancient Celtic monastic site, famous for the many saints said to have been buried on it, including St Deiniol, 6th century bishop of Bangor, and also St Dubricius. The first mention of Augustinians here is in 1252, but they were probably here by c1210. An abbot's house mentioned by Pennant in 1773 seems to have survived until 1814. When the abbey was dissolved in 1537 the choir stalls, two screens and bells are said to have been taken to the newly rebuilt church of Llanengain on the mainland.

The tower of Bardsey Abbey.

BASINGWERK ABBEY   *Cistercian*   SJ 196775   At Greenfield, 2km NE of Holywell

It was probably in 1132 that Ranulf II, Earl of Chester introduced monks of the order of Savigny in this district. The chapel originally assigned for the use of the monks may have been that in the fortified site of Hen Blas 4km to the SE. The monks became Cistercian in 1147 when the order of Savigny was merged with that of Citeaux. They moved to the existing site sometime before 1157, when Henry II granted them a charter and were placed under the supervision of the abbot of Buildwas in Shropshire. An attempt in the next few years towards greater independence was unsuccessful. The monks sided with the English forces in the wars of the late 13th century, there being a record of fifty shillings being paid to the abbey in 1285 in return for one of the monks having celebrated divine services in the castle chapel at Flint. A few years later King Edward allowed the monks to hold a market and fair in nearby Holywell.

A late 15th century description of the abbey refers to it as having roofs of lead and a set of new lodgings to accommodate visitors who were said to be so numerous that meals took two sittings. The abbot at that time was Thomas Pennant who took a wife and resigned his post. His son Nicholas was the last abbot, receiving an annual pension of £17 after surrendering the abbey in 1536. Parts of the church were immediately removed to a church in Chester, and in 1538 the President of the Council of the Marches asked the Lord Privy Seal if the king would allow six fother of lead from the abbey to be used to re-roof the castle at Holt. In 1546 sixty fother of lead from the abbey roofs was taken to Ireland for covering parts of several royal castles, including that of Dublin. In 1540 the site had been granted to Henry ap Harry of Llanasa. It passed by marriage to the Mostyns who held it until it became a monument in state care in 1923.

Of the early 13th century church about 50m long internally there remains only the west wall of the aisled nave of seven bays, the outer wall of the south aisle with a good doorway at its eastern end, the western piers of the crossing and the end wall of the south transept and the outermost of its two square eastern chapels. Just three pier bases remain of the arcades and most of the north side and east end has vanished. Just minor fragments of footings remain of the kitchen with a fireplace at the SW corner of the cloister and of the western range, which was divided from the cloister by a lane, as at the mother house of Buildwas.

The east range of Basingwerk Abbey.

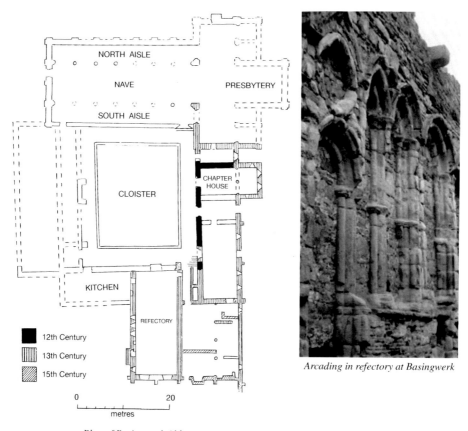

Arcading in refectory at Basingwerk

Plan of Basingwerk Abbey

The eastern parts of the claustral buildings continued to be used after the suppression and are far more complete. Much of the walling enclosing the cloister appears to be 12th century. The east range had a sacristy next to the transept, then a chapter house with a wall-bench and an arcade of two bays leading into a vaulted eastern extension of the 13th century. Next was a passage used as a parlour and then a spacious room used for training novices. There is no sigh of a reredorter serving the dormitory above, but a day stair adjoins the west side. Three of the east windows of the dormitory still survive. A mid 13th century extension of this range contained a warming house with vaults carried on a central row of three piers. In the 15th century the vaulting was removed when the west wall was taken down to widen the room westwards as far as the east wall of the refectory and a fireplace in a projecting bay was provided in the south wall. Extending east from the SE corner of the warming-house is a range of buildings of uncertain date but probably incorporating, or on the site of, parts of the the infirmary or the abbot's house. Running southwards from the cloister south wall, and fairly close to the east range, was a large refectory. It has several lancets in the west wall, plus a pulpit for a meal-time reader, and a serving hatch from the kitchen. There are jambs of two larger windows in the south end wall.

Font at Brecon

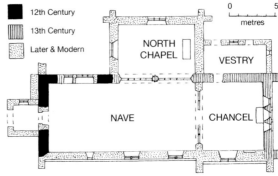

Plan of Beddgelert Priory Church

BASSALEG PRIORY *Benedictine* ST 277872 3km WSW of Newport

Robert de la Haye founded a small priory here c1110 as a cell of Glastonbury Abbey in Somerset. The monks were withdrawn as early as 1235 and nothing so early now survives although the arcade to the south aisle built in 1878 replaced one with "square piers and low arches" which sounds like 12th or early 13th century work. The 15th century east window of the chancel is now the earliest surviving feature.

BEDDGELERT PRIORY *Augustinian* SH 591480 9km NNE of Porthmadoc

In 1188 Gerald of Wales describes the Celtic monastery here as in decline and soon afterwards it became a small Augustinian priory. It was badly damaged by fire c1282, and again in c1432 but survived until 1536, when it had three canons and nine "religious men". The priory buildings probably lay beyond the rebuilt south wall of the church of St Mary. The chancel with a good set of triple east lancets and the finely detailed two bay arcade on the north side of the nave are 13th century. The arcade now opens into a chapel of c1880 which replaced a lost full length aisle. The western part of the nave north wall and the west wall probably predate the Augustinian period.

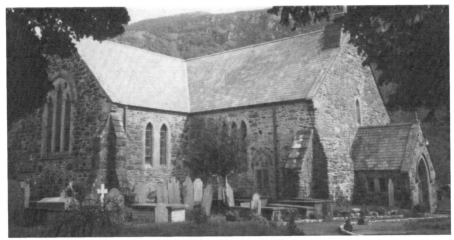

Former priory church of Beddgelert

The choir of Brecon Friary

BRECON FRIARY   *Dominican*   SO 042285   To SW of town centre

The first mention of the friary of St Nicholas lying on the west bank of the Usk just outside the walled town of Brecon is in 1269 but architectural features of the church suggest it was begun c1240. After the friary was suppressed in 1537 the buildings were granted to William Barlow, Bishop of St Davids. In 1541 he transferred the college of Abergwili to this site, which became the College of Christ Church. Here clergymen were trained until a new college was opened further west at Lampeter in 1822. Since 1853 the site has been occupied by a public school which still uses the choir and central passage of the friary church as its chapel. This part is 20m long and has eleven lancets in the north wall. The lancets are original but the wall itself was carefully rebuilt from ground level with the original materials in the 1850s. The east wall has a group of five lancets in a frame occupying almost all of the wall and cannot be earlier than c1300, whilst the tomb recess in the north wall of the sanctuary is of c1320. On the south side is a double piscina and an unusual quadruple set of sedilia.

The central passage area now forms an anti-chapel containing six restored choir stalls of c1400 with misericords carved with figures of a horse, an angel, lions and a skeleton. North of it lies the 14th century chapel of the Awbreys of Abercynrig with a double piscina. This formed the east end of an aisle then added on the north side of the 26m long nave, now ruinous and with the arcade reduced to just the responds. The aisle retains a round-arched north doorway with shallow quadrant mouldings and the nave retains the base of its large west window and a tomb recess on the south side. The cloister on the south side was removed in 1660 and its site is now bisected by a library of 1861. Further south lies a hall created from what was probably the 13th century infirmary, which has an apsidal east end with buttressed corners. The roof of five bays of arch-braced collar-trusses and curved wind-braces is probably 14th century. Projecting from it is a kitchen wing with a pair of shouldered-arched windows facing east. This in turn adjoins a 14th century block now forming the Small Hall but originally probably a guest hall. It has been much rebuilt, including the entire west wall, but retains an original roof of four bays of trusses braced with trefoil arches and large wind-braces also trefoiled.

BRECON PRIORY   *Benedictine*   SO 044290   At the north end of the town

In 1093 the Norman adventurer Bernard de Neufmarche established a new castle at Brecon and gave the church of St John the Evangelist to his confessor Roger, a monk of the newly established abbey at Battle in Sussex. Roger and his companion Walter then set up a priory as a cell of Battle Abbey. Later on it had a prior and eight monks. All that remains of the church built over the next half century is some walling on each side at the east end of the nave and the fine font of the 1130s or 40s with shallow reliefs of grotesque masks alternating with roundels containing birds and beasts. The large cresset stone is also 12th century.

The original cruciform church was gradually rebuilt from 1201 onwards starting with the presbytery, following with the crossing and transepts in the mid 13th century, and then the nave in the 14th century, when it was given aisles with three light windows and a four bay north arcade and north porch and a three bay south arcade. An extra bay at the nave east end has blank walls, although they are pierced with rood-loft staircases rather than solid. The eastern part of the north aisle is the guild chapel of the Corvizors dedicated to St Keyne and retains a fine recess decorated with ballflowers in the outer wall and a screen towards the nave. The eastern arm of the church was of four bays flanked by two bay inner chapels with upper storeys and single bay outer chapels. This layout partly survives on the south side, although the outer chapel has been rebuilt and lengthened and the inner chapel now has its eastern bay divided off as a vestry. On the northern side the chapels have been replaced by the large Harvard Chapel of c1300 with windows of two and three lights. The presbytery has triple sedilia and piscinae on the south side, above which are two pairs of triple lancets, whilst the east end has five lancets, the middle one wider than the others. The intended vaults were not completed because of the patron William de Braose falling from favour with King John and going into exile in 1208, and the existing vaulting is of 1861. Edward Stafford, Duke of Buckingham sponsored the heightening of the central tower c1510-20.

The nave and north transept of Brecon Cathedral

Chapel arches off the south transept at Brecon Cathedral

No actual remains of the cloister survive and the east and south ranges have vanished. A west range extends 35m southwards from the south aisle. Much remodelled in 1927, it has 15th century windows facing east which lighted either a library or a guest house and ends at the south end in four storey tower called the Canonry, which looks early 16th century and has two fireplaces with corbelled lintels and a spiral staircase. Beyond is a narrower extension of c1700. The location of this range allows for a cloister no more than 22m wide. To the SW lies the Deanery, now mostly of the 17th and 19th centuries but with some medieval features. Beyond the west front of the church lies the Almonry. West of it extends a thick curtain wall with a loopholed parapet and a gateway facing north with niches above. It extends to a 17th century tithe barn and then an thinner length of precinct wall extends round the west and south sides of the buildings. A second gateway in it faces west.

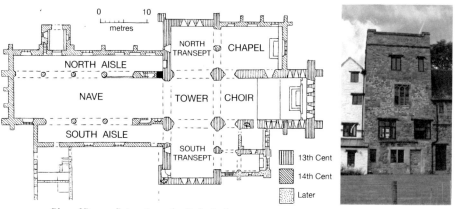

Plan of Brecon Priory (now the Cathedral)

Brecon: The Canonry

Brecon Cathedral from the SE

Chapel screen in Brecon Catthedral

The only medieval monuments at Brecon Cathedral are the slab once dated 1312 with effigies of Walter and Christina Awbrey of Abercynrig and an effigy of a 14th century man in civilian dress in the Harvard chapel. Later monuments include a wooden famale effigy of c1555 of one of the Games family and effigies of Sir David Williams, d1613 and his wife.

Prior's Tower at Caldey Priory

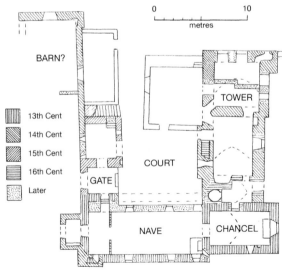

Plan of Caldey Priory

CALDEY PRIORY   *Tironensian*   SS 141963   On an island 4km SSE of Tenby

Caldey Island was granted in 1113 to Robert FitzMartin, lord of Cemaes. He handed it over to his mother Geva, who was the founder of the Tironensian abbey at St Dogmaels which established a cell on the island. Both in the 12th century and in the 1530s just one monk was in residence. In the priory church is a stone with a Latin inscription probably of the 9th century and an Ogham inscription probably of the 6th century referring to Dubracunas. He is said to have consecrated St Sampson as abbot of an early monastery on Caldey c550 in succession to the first abbot called Pyro. Sampson later left to found the monastery at Dol in Brittany. Caldey Island is presently inhabited by about twenty Cistercian monks originally from Chimay in Belgium. The island was purchased in 1928 from what was an originally an Anglo-Catholic community set up in 1900 by Benjamin Fearnly Carlyle who began the present abbey buildings some way to the south of the old priory in 1906. This community converted to Roman Catholicism in 1913 when it had nearly forty members, but got itself into financial difficulties over the expense of constructing all the new buildings.

The old priory is a surprisingly complete group of buildings mostly of 13th to 14th century origin. It had buildings round all sides of a small yard on the north side of a church consisting of a nave with a narrower chancel and a tower with a later stumpy stone spire set over a west porch. A narrow chancel arch leads into the chancel, which has a wide east window, a blocked south window beside a piscina, and a barrel vault probably of the 16th century. The tower has a 14th century west window. The church became a farmhouse in the late 18th century and the north wall was then rebuilt a metre further south. It was restored as a church in the 1890s, when it gained a west gallery.

The derelict east range has next to the church a passage later blocked by the insertion of an oven, then a room with a staircase leading upwards south from a west doorway facing the court. The vault here is probably a 15th century insertion. An upper storey partly oversailing the chancel vault was added in the 16th century. In the 18th and 19th centuries the lower room was used as a dairy and the upper room as a school, both parts having windows of that period. Beyond is an embattled 14th century tower-like block just over 7m square containing a room for the prior over a vaulted basement and having a NE corner projection to contain a latrine off the upper room. There seems to have originally been a staircase turret on the SW corner which was later removed.

Only footings remain of the north range, which appears to have been rebuilt in the 16th or 17th century in a wider form than previously. This part was used for service rooms for the late 18th century mansion of Thomas Kynaston, now demolished. Only the northern end survives of the original west range, which was probably a barn. Between the staircase set against its east wall and the NW corner of the church were later squeezed a service room and an entrance passage to the court with an upper storey over them with a chimney corbelled out of the west wall.

West range of Caldey Priory

Last remains of the Dominican friary at Cardiff

CARDIFF FRIARY   *Dominican*   ST 177770   In Cathays Park, NW of the castle

The currently rather neglected site of the Dominican friary founded by 1242 was excavated c1892. Low and much restored wall-bases delineate a cloister about 26m square with a chapter house at the south end of the east range, a refectory on the north side, and an outer court further north with various buildings including an infirmary at its NE corner. Fragments of mouldings and window tracery suggested a 14th century date for the church on the south side. It had an aisle-less choir 9m wide and 20m long with a sacristy between it and the chapter house. The nave may have originally been of six bays but latterly only had four, with the eastern bay narrower than the others (probably corresponding to the original central walking place), giving a length of 21m.

CARDIFF FRIARY   *Franciscan*   ST 184767   North of the city centre

The street names of The Friary and Greyfriars Road commemorate the site of a Franciscan friary established in the mid 13th century. Part of the site was excavated by the Marquess of Bute in the 1890s. Parts of the buildings may have been incorporated in the fine mansion built on the site by Sir William Herbert c1582, the last remains of which still survived until 1967.

CARDIFF PRIORY   *Benedictine*   ST 182760   North of Cardiff railway station

The existing parish church of St John rebuilt in the 15th century was originally just a chapel-of-ease subservient to the vanished original parish church of St Mary which was founded c1100, and by the 1140s was serving as a priory, being a cell of the Benedictine abbey at Tewkesbury. St Mary's was rebuilt on a cruciform plan in the late 12th century and provided with monastic buildings, but the monks seem to have been withdrawn as early as 1221. By the 16th century the River Taff had developed an oxbow loop which was threatening to undermine the church, and it was abandoned in the 17th century and has gone. The river has since been straightened.

CARDIGAN PRIORY   *Benedictine*   SN 181460   On east side of the town

The church of St Mary originally served a small Benedictine priory founded in the early 12th century by Gilbert de Clare as a cell of Chertsey Abbey in Surrey. After Rhys ap Gruffudd captured Cardigan in 1165 he confirmed the priory's endowments. In the 13th century the church began to attract pilgrims to the see the miraculous taper on the altar of St Mary that burned but was never consumed. It also became the parish church, although originally there seems to have been another church or chapel within the walled town. The church is spacious but lacks aisles. The large west tower was entirely rebuilt in 1711 and 1745-8, having collapsed in 1705. Much of the nave may also be 18th century but the south doorway head and corbelling over the north doorway are 15th century, as is the chancel arch. The chancel has eastern staircase turrets and may be 14th century work with some 15th century remodelling and later restoration. Also 15th century are the font and fragments of old glass in the east window.

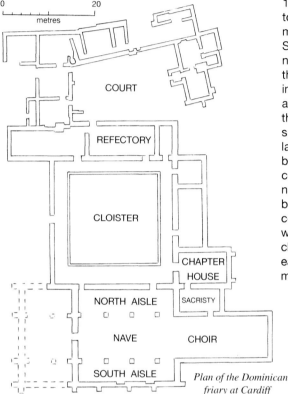

Plan of the Dominican friary at Cardiff

The east range at Caldey Priory

Cardigan Priory Church

CARMARTHEN FRIARY *Franciscan*   SN 411200   In town centre, west of castle

This friary existed by 1282 when William de Valence was buried within the church, whilst in 1284 Edward I visited the town and allowed the friars certain rights over a watercourse supplying a royal mill and the moats of the castle. In 1391 the friars came to an agreement with the prior and convent of St John over the burial of parishioners in the friary church. The friary was surrendered in August 1535 and was immediately stripped of its lead roofs. An inventory of that year refers to the "king's chamber", an inner chamber, a "chamber next to ye lavery", a "chamber next ye parlor dore", a kitchen with an iron range, a brewhouse, hall and buttery. The church had a tower containing a clock and two bells which seems to have survived until the early 19th century. In 1536 Henry VIII handed over the premises to the townspeople for the founding of a grammar school by Thomas Lloyd, "chaunter" of St Davids Cathedral. From the friary church has come the tomb chest in St Peter's Church on which is an effigy of Sir Rhys ap Thomas, d1525 with an heraldic surcoat over his armour, and a smaller female effigy of about the same date, but probably not one of his wives. Another tomb from the friary is that of Edmund Tudor, d1456, now at St Davids. He was Henry VII's father and the grandfather of Henry VIII.

Plan of Carmarthen Friary

Excavations prior to redevelopment of the site in 1998 revealed footings of the refectory on the south side of the main cloister, with three buttresses facing towards a second cloister to the south with alleys on the west, south and east sides and a large southern range (probably the infirmary) with a kitchen in the middle, east of which was a passage leading out to an irregularly shaped latrine wing over a drain. The west wall and several dividing walls were found of the west range of the main cloister, and the NW and SE corners of the chapter house on the east side with a chamber south of it. The church was shown to be about 50m long with a central waking place supporting a tower between the nave and choir. A wide north aisle with an arcade probably of five bays was added in the 15th century.

Former gateway of Carmarthen Augustinian Priory

CARMARTHEN PRIORY *Augustinian*

SN 419204 NE end of town centre

All that remains of the priory is a modest gateway now incorporated in a row of cottages and with the carved Tudor roses noted in 1804 no longer visible. Two late medieval fireplaces and a blocked doorway were revealed on the upper floor in 1993. Excavations in 1979 revealed footings of parts of the church, chapter house and prior's house with fragments of stained glass and glazed tiles of the 15th and 16th centuries. John Speed's map of 1610 shows the church standing in the corner of an enclosure and parts of it stood until Lord Cawdor had the site cleared in 1781 to make way for a lead works. This was once one of the richest monasteries in Wales, with an annual income of just over £200 when it was dissolved in 1536. In the early 12th century Benedictine monks were installed to replace the original Celtic monks, but in 1125 the Benedictines were themselves replaced by Augustinian canons at the instigation of Bishop Bernard of St Davids. The confirmation charter from Henry I mentions the church as being dedicated to St John the Evangelist and St Theuloc, the latter probably actually meant to be St Teulyddog and confirmation of the presence of an early monastery here.

The west front of Chepstow Priory Church

The north side of Chepstow Priory Church

CHEPSTOW PRIORY   *Benedictine*   ST 536930   On east side of the town

A small priory dependent on the abbey of Cormeilles in Normandy was founded either by William Fitz-Osbern, Earl of Hereford, d1071, or by his son Roger de Breteuil shortly afterwards. The priory fell on hard times in the 14th century and lay empty from 1394 to 1398 when fresh monks were sent over from Bermondsey, but it recovered later. The eastern part of the church probably completed in the 1090s was destroyed after the suppression in 1536 but five out of the six bays of the early 12th century nave remain in the present parish church of St Mary. The nave has a very fine west doorway of five orders with chevrons on the inner and outer arches and on the blind arches on either side. Above are three windows in a similar style with billets on the arches. The arcades are of two orders on rectangular piers. The triforium above has just plain round-arched openings but on the (presumably slightly later) south side there are paired shafted arches with shafted sub-arches. There is also an original clerestory. There were once shafts dividing the bays and vaults with cells of tufa blocks between oolite stone ribs. One of the two fonts (that the south aisle) is also Norman work. See photos on page 37.

The original transepts survived until the fall of the central tower in 1701. The crossing was then walled off and a new tower built within the west bay of the nave, the lower parts of it being re-used Norman material. A new scheme providing fresh transepts was begun in 1838. This resulted in the loss of the Norman work in the eastern bay of the nave. Worse still, the high vault was taken down and the filling of the nave with galleries allowed the demolition of the aisles. In the 1890s the galleries were removed and the transepts divided off from the crossing by two bay arcades, that on the north side with the pier perched on the base of the original NW pier of the Norman central tower. A new vestry was added on the north side of the chancel, which was lengthened. One bay of the south aisle was reinstated before work came to a halt in 1913. The oldest of the many monuments are the recumbent effigies of Henry, 2nd Earl of Worcester, d1549, and his second wife Elizabeth, and a recumbent effigy of Margaret Clayton, d1627, with her two husbands kneeling behind and her twelve children against the dado below.

Excavations in 1973-4 found remains of a cloister of irregular shape resulting from east and west ranges being built at an awkward angle to the church in the early 12th century. The east range contained a chapter house with presumably a dormitory above. A south range containing a refectory was added c1240 and given a fireplace in a remodelling c1500, when the west range was rebuilt slightly further west to provide a new prior's house. Remains were also found of a barn to the SW.

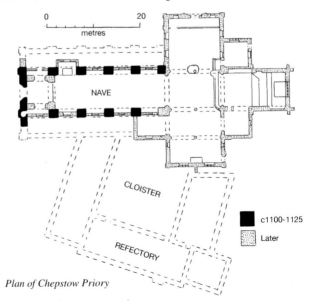

Plan of Chepstow Priory

CWM HIR ABBEY   *Cistercian*   SO 055711   10km north of Llandrindod Wells

According to the Chronicle of Chester Abbey this abbey was originally founded in 1143 by Maredudd, son of Madoc ap Idwerth. His brothers Cadwallon and Einion Clud re-founded it with monks from Whitland in 1176. It then prospered and a huge new church was begun in the 1190s and continued into the 1220s under patronage from Llywelyn Fawr. His grandson Llywelyn ap Gruffydd was buried here in 1282. Work on the buildings may have stopped in 1231 when the abbey was threatened with destruction by the forces of Henry III of England after part of them were lured into a trap by someone connected with the abbey. Only payment of a very heavy fine lifted the threat. The abbey also suffered at the hands of Owain Glyndwr in 1403. When the abbey was suppressed in 1536 its lands were worth just £28 per annum and there were just three monks left.

The site is an oddly cramped one in a small valley. The nearby village is known as Abbey Cwmhir and so by default also are the ruins. Nothing is now visible of the claustral buildings. If it had ever been completed the church here would have been the largest in Wales with an internal length of not less than 100m. The fully aisled fourteen bay long nave which was completed was 76m long internally and 10.5m wide across the main body, and 21m wide including the aisles. Of it there remain most of the south wall dado, featureless apart from four shaft bases and gaps for doorways at the east end and in the third bay from the west, together with fragments of the base of the north wall built against higher ground and bases of two piers on the south side and one pier on the north. The lower parts of the west walls of transepts also remain, but there is uncertainty as to whether anything further east was ever built. From this church has come the five bay arcade in the parish church of Llanidloes 16km to the NE, clumsily re-erected there in the 1540s with the piers shorter than originally. The piers have fine stiff-leaf capitals and are formed of eight groups of three shafts with the middle one filleted set on a square core set diagonally and the arches have complex roll mouldings.

Part of an arcade from Cwm Hir now at Llanidloes parish church

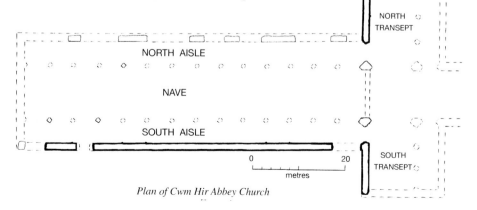

NORTH TRANSEPT

NORTH AISLE

NAVE

SOUTH AISLE

SOUTH TRANSEPT

0   20

metres

Plan of Cwm Hir Abbey Church

Remains of sedilia in Cymer Abbey

CYMER ABBEY   *Cistercian*   SH 722195   2km NNE of Dolgellau

From a confirmation charter granted by Llywelyn Fawr in 1209 it appears that this abbey was founded by Gruffydd ap Cynan and his bother Maredudd and his son Hywell, monks for it being sent over from the abbey of Cwm Hir in 1198. The abbey held lands in the neighbouring parishes of Llanelltyd, Llanegryn, Llanfachreth and Trawsfynydd, but about a fifth of its meagre income came from the grange of Neigwl on the Lleyn peninsula. The estates were worth only £12 in the taxation list of 1291, partly because the revenues from Neigwl were then being withheld by Dafyd ap Gruffydd, but the lands were valued at over £51 when the abbey was suppressed and the buildings passed to the Vaughans of Nannau. The ruin has been a monument in state care since 1930.

Like other abbeys founded by Welsh princes, and especially the mother house at Cwm Hir, the buildings were completed in the mid 13th century to a much reduced plan than that originally envisaged. Low walls mark out a cloister 22m square with a long single room on the south side which was probably subdivided into a kitchen and refectory. The doorway on the east side of the cloister led into a chapter house projecting beyond the east range which must have had a rere-dorter at the south end flushed by the drain running under the south range. There are no traces of a western range for lay-brothers. They may not have been an important part of this community. The cloister has just a wide western doorway looking like an entrance and the church as completed does not seem to allow room for a separate lay-brothers' choir.

North of cloister lies what was intended as just the nave of the church, but the transepts, crossing and presbytery as planned were never built. Instead a wall was built across the east end of the nave with three lancets for the main body and a single lancet for the north aisle. No other windows remain. An arcade of three bays remains at the west end on the north side. Otherwise there were solid walls between the nave and the aisles apart from a doorway on each side. The south aisle of the church may in fact never have been roofed and used as such. The nave has a south doorway corresponding to the easternmost arcade arch on the north. Between this doorway and the doorways further east lay the monks' choir. On the south side east of the doorway are a set of three rather damaged sedilia, then a gap for a tomb recess, and then a piscina. There is another tomb recess on the north side. The north aisle also retains a piscina. In the 14th century a diagonally buttressed tower was added at the west end. It has a loop on each of the north, west and south sides and a staircase in the SW corner. The upper parts have not survived, and may in any case have been timber-framed.

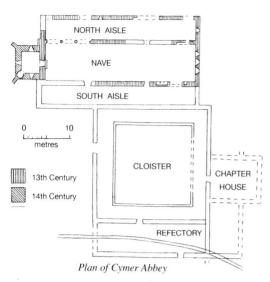

Plan of Cymer Abbey   *North arcade at Cymer Abbey*

DENBIGH FRIARY   *Carmelite*   SJ 060666   At NE end of lower part of the town

Probably about the same time as the upper town was walled in the 1280s a friary was founded at the far end of the lower town. Major patrons included Sir John Salisbury of Llewenny, who was buried here in 1289, and John de Sunimore. The choir of the church remained in use as a malthouse with the original roof surviving until a fire in 1898. Ruins survive of a building 7.5m wide and about 19m long with a bricked up 15th century east window of five lights. Normally the choir alone of a friary would be about this length but the western part of what remains must have formed the east end of the nave since there is below a south window a second piscina for a nave SE altar 13m from the east wall. The doorway east of it must have admitted to the central walking place, over which was a timber-framed tower. There are three sedilia beside the easternmost piscina. The north side has remains of a window of five lights. To the south, across a garden on the site of the cloister, lies a house containing remains of the dormitory range with two doorways. In the garden is the indent of a brass of a priest. An inventory of the friary possessions mentions a chapter house and a chamber for the bishop (of St Asaph) on the east side of the cloister, a hall, buttery and chamber on the west, and also a kitchen, another chamber, a gatehouse and an
orchard and garden.

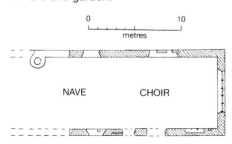

Plan of Denbigh friary church   *Looking eastwards into Denbigh Friary*

EWENNY PRIORY   *Benedictine*   SS 912779   2km SSE of Bridgend

Sometime in the 1120s William de Londres, whose seat was the castle at Ogmore, built a church at Ewenny and gave possession of it to the Benedictine abbey of Gloucester. In 1141 William's son Maurice donated other gifts to provide the endowment for a priory for twelve monks and a prior at Ewenny. The well-preserved church must date from about that time and the vanished claustral buildings must have been substantially complete by the mid 13th century. Patronage must then have dried up since the descendants of the heiress Hawise de Londres occupied the castle of Kidwelly in preference to Ogmore. An effigy of Hawise and cross-slabs from the tombs of her father and grandfather are amongst the many memorial fragments in the south transept. At the suppression the nave (except its walled-off western end) remained in use as a parish church, the outer wall of its north aisle then being rebuilt and given a new porch. They were rebuilt again in 1895. The eastern parts of the church passed into private hands but remained roofed as a burial place. They passed into state care in 1949.

The church of St Michael consists of a nave five bays long with an arcade of four round arches on circular piers on the north side, a central crossing with transepts each with two east chapels, and a presbytery ending in a sanctuary with one window on each side and three facing east.

The nave has round arched windows high up on both sides, those on the south being above where the north alley of the cloister abutted the other side. The lower part of the western arch of the crossing is filled with a 13th century screen wall against which was placed the parochial altar, as now. The southern doorway through the screen wall is original but the other doorway is a later insertion.

The south transept at Ewenny Priory   *Graveslab at Ewenny Priory*

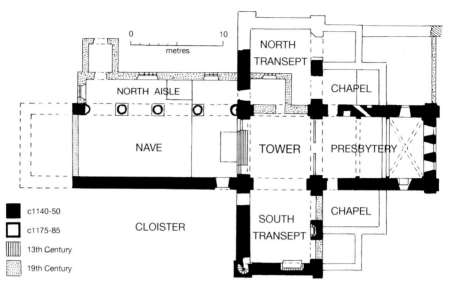

Plan of Ewenny Priory Church

The eastern parts have clasping corner buttresses of good ashlar. The inner chapels were longer than the outer ones and had doorways connecting them with the presbytery. On the south side the chapels have gone and the arches to them are walled up. A small modern vestry occupies the southern part of the north transept. The rest of it, including both chapels, has since c1800 been reduced to the lower parts of the walls. The inner chapel here had a squint through the presbytery wall towards the high altar. The interior has a string-course adorned with chevrons, above which level the crossing piers have pairs of shafts. The sanctuary is covered with a rib-vault and the other two bays of the presbytery have a plain barrel-vault with a transverse rib. The screen now dividing off the presbytery has a 14th century top and 16th century lower parts and has been moved from the nave, where it originally divided off the eastern bay.

The south transept end wall has a later medieval tomb recess, and three windows, the middle one set over the lower two. Unusually the gable of the dormitory over the east range of the claustral buildings did not reach quite as far north as this wall. The doorway high up over the chapel arches led into a chamber over the chapel vaults, probably a later addition. In the SW corner of the transept a spiral stair leads up to a passage leading to the tower. Towards the transept the passage has an arcade of small arches on short columns with cubical capitals. The tower over the crossing has restored battlements of c1300 with crossloops.

Arch into the inner north chapel at Ewenny

Ewenny: north tower of precinct wall

The north arcade at Ewenny

The east range of the claustral buildings has vanished but parts of the south and west ranges survive in the present house. There is a thirteenth century window at the north end of the west range. The Carne family made a grand house here in the 17th century.

The church lies in the NE corner of a precinct enclosed by a high embattled wall which looks like a defensive structure although its provision was probably more a matter of prestige. The vulnerable east side is not embattled. The wall is now missing between the rectangular SE tower and the south gatehouse, although the Buck brothers' engraving of 1741 still shows it complete. The outer part of the gateway passage is late 12th century. It is flanked on the east side by a 7m wide tower of c1300 with the outer part polygonal on a spurred base. This gateway was made into a summer-house in the 19th century. From this gate all the way round past the circular NW tower to the north gatehouse the wall is very complete, with both a wall-walk and parapet with loops in the merlons. The NW tower is open-gorged and has two levels of cross-loops. The north gate is an impressive building of c1300 about 9m wide with chamfered outer corners and a portcullis groove in the passage, the inner part of which is late 12th century work. A spiral stair on the east side leads to the upper storey. East of here the wall passes a barn. There is then a gap before reaching the ruinous north tower of c1300. The section from there around the parochial cemetery in the NE corner is now missing. At some time the east wall of the precinct was joined to the north transept northern chapel by a cut-off wall.

GOLDCLIFF PRIORY   *Benedictine*   ST 372820   By coast, 9km SE of Newport

In 1113 Robert de Chandos founded a priory here for a prior and twelve monks by the shore of the Severn estuary as a cell of the abbey of Bec in Normandy. In 1295 it had 25 monks and estates in across the estuary in Devon and Somerset. The priory was badly affected by extensive flooding in 1424. The connection with Bec was severed in 1442 and it became a cell of the abbey of Tewkesbury but the last monks left in 1467. The existing parish church further inland to the NW was built just after the flood of 1424, the squared limestone blocks in the south and west walls being probably reused from the older building, which has otherwise vanished.

The vaulted sanctuary at Ewenny Priory

GRACE DIEU ABBEY *Cistercian* Uncertain location 5km west of Monmouth

Monks arrived here in 1226 from Abbey Dore in Herefordshire, although the endowment dated back to 1217. The community transferred to a new location in 1236. It remained the poorest of all Cistercian houses in England and Wales and had just two monks when suppressed in 1536. The Herberts of Wonastow acquired the lands. Nothing remains visible of the buildings.

HAVERFORDWEST FRIARY *Dominican* SN 954156 East side of town centre

Little is known about this friary of St Saviour originally founded in 1246 but moved c1256 to a new site east of Bridge Street, on which occasion Henry III donated 15 merks to the friars.

Haverfordwest Priory

HAVERFORDWEST PRIORY   *Augustinian*   SM 957152   To SE of town centre

Robert Fitz-Richard is thought to have founded this priory c1200, but from 1213 much of its patronage must come from William Marshal, d1219, and his four sons who succeeded him each in turn. There are few mentions of the priory in the chronicles and records. Its lands must have suffered from Welsh attacks in 1220 and 1405 although there is no mention of the buildings being damaged. Much of its revenue came from the three parish churches in the town and rents from properties adjoining the priory just outside the town walls, but it also held the manor of Cokey and had a grange at Green, both fairly nearby. After being suppressed in 1536 the priory site was acquired by the Barlow family. They later did an exchange for land at Slebech with Sir John Perrot, who is thought to have taken material from the priory buildings for works at his house nearby at Haroldston. The ruin has been in state care since 1982.

Recent excavations have shown that the site beside the Cleddau needed considerable levelling to build it up sufficiently for flooding not to be a constant problem. As laid out in the early 13th century on the platform thus created, the priory consisted of a simple aisle-less cruciform church 46m long internally with a cloister 23m square on the south side with ranges round the other three sides. The presbytery walls needed a higher base and more support than the other parts, with heavy clasping buttresses on the eastern corners. Very little fine detail now remains anywhere on the site and the transepts are the only parts to stand much above the wall bases. Most of the rest was buried until a few years ago. The south and west fringes of the site have yet to be fully cleared but the herb gardens beyond the east range have now been recreated. These gardens seem to have been a late medieval feature replacing a former cemetery.

There are two rather damaged lancets in the north transept west wall. The south transept retains an altar base and a nearby piscina and a single sedile, plus the base of the night stair down from the adjoining dormitory. The canons' stalls filled the crossing area and screens behind them blocked the transept arches, necessitating passages behind the east responds of the arches. West of here in the eastern part of the nave a tower was raised in the late medieval period. Other late medieval alterations included a new cloister arcade supporting roofs sloping down to drain into gullies in the central garden, a vault provided in the chapter house in the east range, and an extra room added beside the south side of the east end of the chapter house. There was originally a tomb with an effigy of a knight in the chapter house, the head of the figure being found in the excavations. There was a reredorter at the south end of the dormitory. The detached building further south is thought to have been the infirmary. The south range contained the refectory with a readers pulpit on the south side, but the eastern end also contained the day stair to the dormitory. Beside the refectory doorway in the cloister is a lavatory recess. The building south of here is thought to have been the kitchen. Four doorways lead from the western cloister alley into the west range but the range itself has yet to be fully cleared and conserved.

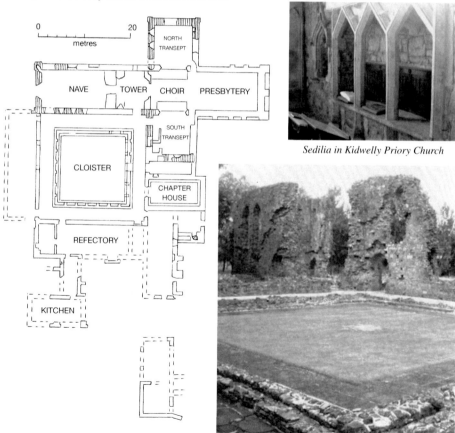

Sedilia in Kidwelly Priory Church

Plan of Haverfordwest Priory

Haverfordwest Priory

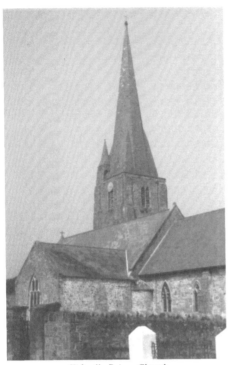

Kidwelly Priory Church

KIDWELLY PRIORY   *Benedictine*
SN 409068 In middle of village,

Roger, Bishop of Sarum (Salisbury) founded this priory c1110. It normally had just a prior and one or two other monks, who were always of English origin, rather than Welsh. In 1284 the archbishop of Canterbury, John Pecham, a former Franciscan friar, visited the priory and sent prior Ralph de Bemenster back in disgrace to the mother house of Sherborne in Dorset. The archbishop was outraged when the abbot of Sherborne re-appointed Ralph as prior and sent him back to Kidwelly. The church was hit by lightning in October 1481 and it was possibly then that the west end of the nave was destroyed. The priory was excused from tithe payments in 1513 and 1517 on account of its poverty. A few years afterwards the Bishop of St Davids ordered the tithes to be used for repairing the choir of the church and the prior's house.

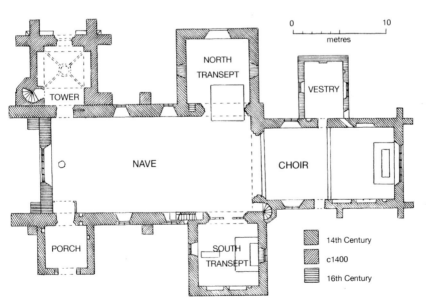

Plan of Kidwelly Priory Church

The choir of Kidwelly Priory

Because of its status as a cell of Sherborne the priory was not suppressed until the mother house was closed in 1539, when Prior John Painter was granted an annual pension of £8. The church remained in parochial use but the other priory buildings were leased to the wine merchants George Aysshe and Robert Myryk. Nothing now remains apart from the church but the late 13th or 14th century prior's house with a corbelled upper storey and a thatched roof survived into the early 20th century.

In its present shortened form the crucifom church is 37m long internally. Most of it is 14th century, dating from when the castle was held by the Earl of Lancaster, but the thick walls of the 10m wide nave could be partly 12th century and the chancel arch piers look like 13th century work on older bases. The vestry has a squint towards the high altar, and must represent a remodelled or replaced chantry chapel. Both the nave and choir have two-light windows but the east window is of five lights. The choir has a piscina and a triple set of sedilia (see p47). Over the high altar is a 14th century figure of the Virgin. There is no crossing as such but the position of a rood-loft staircase on the south side indicates that the eastern part of the nave was screened off for the use of the monks. The south transept has a blocked east window and two tomb recesses, one with a floriated cross slab and the other with a slab with a female mask. A damaged effigy lies nearby. The north transept also has two blocked windows. Both the south porch and the fine porch tower of c1400 on the north side overlap the present west wall in which is a five-light window of c1500. The tower is heavily buttressed and contains a vault and supports a slender spire, most of which is a 19th century rebuilding.

LLANDAFF CATHEDRAL   *Secular Canons*   ST 156781   4km NW of Cardiff

In 1120 Urban, the second Norman bishop, began to build a new cathedral to replace a small building with low aisles and an apse that had previously served the Celtic monastery here. The dedication is to St Peter and St Paul, together with the Celtic saints Dyfrig, Teilo and Euddogwy. All that remains of Urban's church is the sanctuary arch behind the present high altar and some walling on the south side of the choir, where there survive the heads of two round-arched windows. The arch is of five orders, two of them decorated with chevrons and the outer one with beaded medallions enclosing eight-petalled flowers. Medallions were a feature of contemporary work at Malmsbury Abbey and Sarum Cathedral, making it likely that the Sarum masons worked on this job.

Of the late 12th century are the reset north and south doorways in the outer walls. The north doorway is of Sutton stone and is narrower than the south doorway of Dundry stone. Both doorways feature scallop capitals and chevrons and the north doorway has dogtooth on a hoodmould ending with animal head-stops.

The west front and the western four bays of the nave date from the time of Bishop Henry of Abergavenny from 1193 to 1218. He established the cathedral chapter in its present form with four dignitaries and nine other canons. Unusually, the bishop presided over the chapter until deans began to be appointed in 1840. Begun probably c1205, the work again shows the influence of buildings in the West Country of England, with recent designs at Glastonbury Abbey and Wells Cathedral being the models. The west front is very impressive with three lancets with internal detached shafts over a single doorway with twin round arches, and a topmost window flanked externally by blind arcading. However the overall design is modest for a cathedral since it lacks a triforium. It did include provision for two west towers, although the existing towers are of much later date. When another four bays further east with more slender piers and arcades were built in the 1220s under Bishop William de Goldcliff no provision was made for a crossing or transepts. However, a square chapter house, vaulted in four bays with a central pier, and with a lancet window in each bay and a rebuilt upper room, was built on the south side, facing a slope. Between the chapter house and the sanctuary one bay of the south aisle is vaulted, possibly with the intention of raising a tower over it.

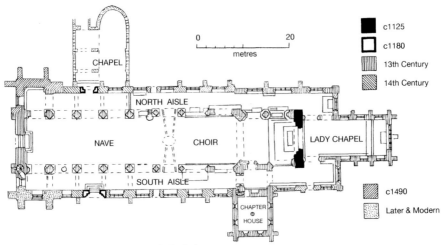

Plan of Llandaff Cathedral

In the late 13th century the presbytery was remodelled, with two new arches on each side. The original sanctuary was then replaced by a Lady Chapel five bays long with a five-light east window and two-light side windows. Shafts with water-holding bases and stiff-leaf capitals support a rib-vault. The window shafts are of Purbeck marble. The east ends of the choir aisle were rebuilt so as to flank the first two bays of the Lady Chapel. Also probably of that period is the fragmentary stump of a huge bell-tower 13m square at the top of the slope high above the south side of the cathedral. Further east lies the ruin of the castle built c1280-87 by Bishop William de Braose. It has a fine twin-towered gatehouse at one corner of a modest rectangular court.

The west front of Llandaff Cathedral

The outer walls of the rest of the aisles were rebuilt in the 14th century, mostly with three-light windows with a variety of tracery forms, but with one five-light window just east of the chapter house. There is no proof that the NW tower was sponsored by Jasper Tudor, Duke of Bedford and lord of Glamorgan from 1485 to 1495 but it certainly dates from about that time. It is of three stages with boldly projecting set-back buttresses. The Somerset-type openwork crown was entirely rebuilt in the mid 19th century the design being based on that at St John's church at Cardiff.

The cathedral soon deteriorated after the Reformation. Services were suspended in 1692 because of the state of the roofs. The NW tower lost its parapet in a gale in 1703 and the SW tower completely collapsed in 1722. The choir and east bays of the nave were remodelled in a temple-like form in the 1740s, whilst the western four bays of the nave remained in ruins for over a century. Restoration of the Lady Chapel began in 1841 and the remainder was brought back into use during the 1850s and 60s, culminating with the rebuilding of the SW tower with a tall spire in 1867-9. Considerable further rebuilding took place in the 1950s to repair damage caused by a land mine that exploded just outside the south aisle during a raid by German bombers in 1941. The blast destroyed all the roofs, parapets and window tracery on that side. It was during the rebuilding that Jacob Epstein's Majestas statue was placed high upon concrete parabolic arches in the middle of the building, forming a division between the nave and choir that the cathedral had previously lacked. A concrete-walled chapel of St David was also added on the north side outside the Late Norman doorway there.

Tomb in the choir of Llandaff Cathedral

Probably the earliest of the many monuments at Llandaff is an effigy of a bishop in flat relief in the Lady Chapel, claimed (but unlikely) to be William de Braose, d1287. In the nave are effigies thought to be Bishop Henry of Abergavenny, d1218, and Bishop William de Radnor, d1265, plus effigies of Sir William Mathew, d1528 and his wife with monks, ladies and shield-bearing angels on their tomb chest. Another 13th century bishop has his effigy on the sanctuary south side, unless the effigy is meant to be of St Teilo. The head is surmounted by a trefoiled and shafted canopy held by angels. Another 13th century effigy of a bishop lies in the north choir aisle along with effigies of Sir David Mathew, d1461, Bishop John Marshal, d1496, and Sir Christopher Mathew, d1526 and his wife. The medieval reredos there must have originally been behind the high altar. Other interesting medieval relics are the rare late 15th century tester incorporated into the sedilia of the St Euddogwy Chapel, showing Bishop Marshal kneeling by the Adoration of the Virgin, and a late 15th century German relief in the south aisle probably from an altarpiece and showing the Dormition of the Virgin.

LLANFAES FRIARY   *Franciscan*   SH 606774   1.5km NNE of Beaumaris

When Princess Joan, daughter of King John of England, died in 1237 she was buried in the church of a Franciscan friary newly founded by her husband Llywelyn Fawr which was consecrated in 1245. The church had triple east lancets and survived in use as a barn until 1819, when it was demolished. Other remnants of the friary incorporated in a house of the Wynn or Whyte family survived until site clearance for building the present house called Fryars in 1866. Llanfaes was a town in the 13th century with 120 burgages and thus able to support a community of mendicant friars. In the 1290s the town was suppressed in favour of the new royal castle and fortified town of Beaumaris, the Welsh inhabitants of Llanfaes being sent down to Newborough. Princess Joan's coffin with a bust of a female figure set on a floriated stem on the lid has ended up in the porch of the 14th century parish church at Beaumaris, which also has a good set of choir stalls with misericords probably from Llanfaes. The very fine tomb with effigies of Gronw Fychan, d1382, and his wife Myfanwy once in the friary church has ended up in the parish church at Penmynydd lying 2.5km east of their house at Plas Penynydd.

LLANFAIR PRIORY *Benedictine*

SN 764341   NE of Llandovery

The parish church of St Mary set within a former Roman fort is a wide single chamber with its western part dating from the sixty years up until 1185, when the cell here of the priory of Malvern in Worcestershire was closed. The nave retains one 12th century window on each side. The east end is 13th century and internally has the stumps of two east lancets, their bases buried by a later medieval raising of the sanctuary floor level. The west tower with a vaulted base is probably late 14th century. On the south side is a blocked arch for a former south chapel, probably of the 15th century. There are hints that the church may have had transepts by the end of the 13th century.

Llangennith Church

LLANGENNITH PRIORY *Benedictine*   SS 429914   In village at W end of Gower

St Cennydd is said to have had a hermitage here in the 6th century. In the early 12th century the church was given by Henry, Earl of Warwick to the abbey of St Taurin at Evreux, and a cell then established composed of just a prior and one other monk. It was amongst the several alien priories suppressed by Henry V in 1414. The two south doorways now obscured by a raising of the floor level in the 1880s probably communicated with the vanished priory buildings. In the medieval lordship of Gower only the town of Swansea had a larger church than that Llangennith, which has a notably wide and long 13th century nave and a narrower chancel, both probably 13th century. The rectangular north transeptal tower also looks 13th century because of its paired lancets and saddleback roof with corbelled parapets to north and south. However the blocked round-headed east arch to a former chapel or apse suggests the lower part may be Norman. Of the 14th century are the chancel east window, the recumbent effigy of a formerly cross-legged knight of the de la Mare family, and probably the north porch. On the west wall is a fragment of a 9th century cross-shaft with interlace.

LLANLLUGAN ABBEY *Cistercian Nuns*   SJ 058022   12km NW of Newtown

A meadow on the north bank of the River Rhiw is assumed to be the site of a Cuistercian nunnery founded before 1188 by Maredudd ap Rhotpert, Lord of Cedewain, and suppressed in 1536. It was supervised by the abbot of Strata Florida. Four nuns and an abbess are recorded here in 1377. A figure of an abbess appears together with a crucifix and an effigy of a klng on 15th century stained glass in the parish church higher up to the north. The font there goes back to c1200 and the roof is 14th or 15th cenrtury.

LLANTARNAM ABBEY *Cistercian*   ST 311930   4km NW of Caerleon

The community established in 1179 by Hywel ap Iorwerth, the Welsh lord of Caerleon was originally called Caerleon Abbey and may have been closer to that place until a transfer to Llantarnam in the late 13th century. Of that latter period there survives a roofless ivy-clad barn eleven bays long to the NW of the present house of the 1830s. Part of the barn north wall is held up with flying buttresses. The house replaced one built out of the monastic buildings after their purchase in 1554 by William Morgan of Caerleon.

LLANTHONY PRIORY   *Augustinian*   SO 289279   14km north of Abergavenny

In 1103 a priest called Ernisius visited the hermit William de Lacy here and decided to join him. William had found a ruined chapel in this isolated spot and had decided to retire here for a life of study and contemplation. The two soon gathered followers and invited canons from newly founded Augustinian houses to come over and instruct them. By c1118 the community at Llanthony had become an Augustinian priory with Ernisius as prior and Hugh de Lacy as the patron. They were aided by gifts from Henry I and from Queen Matilda, whom Ernisius had once served as chaplain. By the end of the 1130s Henry's I peaceful reign had ended and the Welsh were threatening the area. The canons sought temporary refuge at Hereford with the bishop there but were then given land by Gloucester to set up what was intended to be just a cell of the original house.

The de Lacy family recovered their position in the 1150s and persuaded some of the canons to return to the original Llanthony and build a new church there, which was eventually 64m long internally. The crossing and transepts each with one east chapel and a presbytery three bays long were begun in the 1170s and probably complete by c1200, after which work was begun on a fully aisled nave eight bays long with a fine west doorway and rectangular towers over the western bays of the aisles. Both these towers still stand high and the west and south sides of the central tower also remain. The north arcade survives complete with a clerestory of twinned lancets above it, but only pier bases remain of the middle four bays of the south arcade following their collapse in 1837, and the outer walls of the aisles have gone. The chapels off the transepts were rebuilt larger in the late 13th century but in later times the north one was abandoned. The west window fell in 1803, and the east window had then also recently gone.

By the early 13th century work was underway on a cloister 27m square and ranges all around it. Only part of the north wall remains of the refectory on the south side. About half of the western range with vaulted cellars and an outer parlour next the church SW tower survives in a hotel. Of the eastern range there survives the lower parts of a slype or passage next to the transept and a large chapter house with a polygonal east end. After the suppression the infirmary hall with its three blocked doorways became the nave of a parish church of St David (across the road to the south) using the infirmary chapel as a chancel. Originally the nave windows rose above present eaves level. To the south is a ruined circular dovecote and to the west is a gatehouse made into a barn.

An old view of Llanthony Priory from the NE

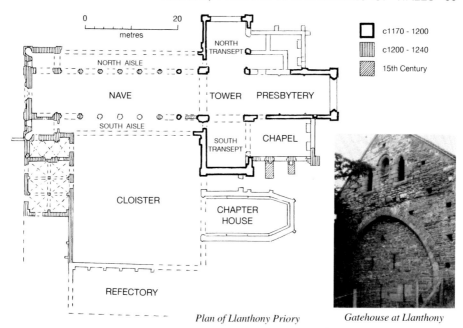

Plan of Llanthony Priory   Gatehouse at Llanthony

Most of what now stands of the priory must have been complete by the time Walter de Lacy died in 1241 and his inheritance was divided amongst heiresses. In 1274 there is a record of three of the canons being at large after fleeing from the priory, and in 1276 Edward I placed one of his clerks in charge of the priory because it was in debt. In 1279 a quarrel with a neighbour led to an incident in which two canons were killed, their prior was wounded, and some of the priory's cattle were driven off. In 1362 a similar quarrel resulted in the prior and two canons leading a band of men in a raid on a manor house at Holme Lacy and the destruction of a new weir across the River Wye and sluices off it to a mill. In 1404 Henry IV notified his officers in Ireland, where Llanthony had considerable estates donated by the de Lacy lords of Meath, that the prior was a loyal subject in difficulties because his priory was then surrounded by followers of Owain Glyndwr. In the following year it was necessary to store some of the priory's goods in Hereford for safety. The community never recovered from this hiatus combined with the effects of poor management of its affairs. 1481 Edward IV allowed a form of unification with Llanthony Secunda at Gloucester with the provision that a prior and four canons were to remain here at the original Llanthony. Both houses survived being suppressed until as late as March 1538. Prior David of the original Llanthony and his four canons were granted pensions of £8 each. The priory and most of its estates in England and Wales went to Nicholas Arnolde. It was later sold to the Harleys, then to the Wood family and in c1807 again to Walter Savage Landor. The ruins have been in state care since 1951.

MALPAS PRIORY *Cluniac* ST 302901 2km NNW of Newport

Just one head corbel in the vestry remains of the original church begun c1110 to serve a cell of the Cluniac priory of Montacute in Somerset. The existing neo-Norman church of St Mary is of 1849-50. Old drawings suggest that the elaborate west doorway and chancel arch are similar to (if not copies of) the 12th century originals.

MARGAM ABBEY   *Cistercians*   SS 791863   6km SE of Port Talbot

The Celtic monastery here was extinguished in 1147 when Robert, Earl of Gloucester, lord of Glamorgan granted lands here to the abbey of Clairvaux, then ruled by St
Bernard, for the foundation of a daughter house. The abbey lay beside the old Roman
coast road out to west Wales used as a route to St Davids and beyond to Ireland by
Henry in 1170-71 and King John in 1210. The latter was well entertained at Margam
and as a result spared the abbey (and his own new foundation at Beaulieu) from a harsh
tax imposed upon all the English and Welsh Cistercian houses as a retaliation for their
tardiness in providing funds for his recent campaign in Ireland.

Margam was one of the wealthiest Welsh abbeys although its income suffered in certain years through Welsh attacks on its properties and natural disasters. In 1336, when
the abbey had 38 monks and 40 lay brothers, it was said to be unable to pay its debts
as the estates had recently suffered from warfare, plagues and sand invasions (to which
its properties at Kenfig were particularly vulnerable). In 1384 the abbey was granted the
tithes of several churches to help its financial position but the depredations of Owain
Glyndwr's supporters again reduced the monks to straightened circumstances.

The abbey had an annual income of £181 when in 1536 it was surrendered by the
last nine monks under their abbot Lewis Thomas, who was granted a pension of £20.
The buildings and most of the lands were then acquired by Sir Rice Mansel of Oxwich
and Old Beaupre, d1559, whose effigy, together with those of Sir Edward, d1585, and
Sir Thomas (and their wives) fill the SE chapel of the church. By the late 16th century the
family had incorporated parts of the south and west ranges of the claustral buildings
into a fine mansion which became their main seat. Their successors the Talbots briefly
transferred to Penrice on the Gower. The Margam house was demolished in the 1770s
to be replaced by a fine orangery of 1787-90, whilst a new house was built further east
in 1830s when they returned from the Gower. The estate has been a country park
owned by West Glamorgan county council since 1973. There is currently no direct access between the monastic ruins in the park and the churchyard containing the church
and the Stones Museum in which is a superb collection of Early Christian crosses.

The church eventually attained an internal length of 80m
and consisted of an aisled nave eight bays long, a crossing
probably with a tower, transepts each with two east chapels, and a fully aisled presbytery of five bays. The western
six bays of the nave of c1160-80 remain in use as the parish church of St Mary. The east wall and the outer walls of
the aisles with their plaster groin-vaults are of the restoration of c1805-10. The central part of the west front with the
doorway and pilaster buttress-turrets behind the arcade
responds is original but the aisle end walls, the tops of the
turrets, the rings on the shafts of the doorway and the three
windows above it are not, although the old and new parts
are both of Sutton stone and merge quite well. The arcades
are of two square orders of round arches set on rectangular
piers. There are no medieval furnishings or monuments left
in the church, but the stones museum contains three 13th
century grave slabs, plus another to Robert, Abbot of Riev-
aulx, who died at Margam in 1307, and also the lower part
of a cross-legged 14th century knight.

South aisle at Margam Abbey

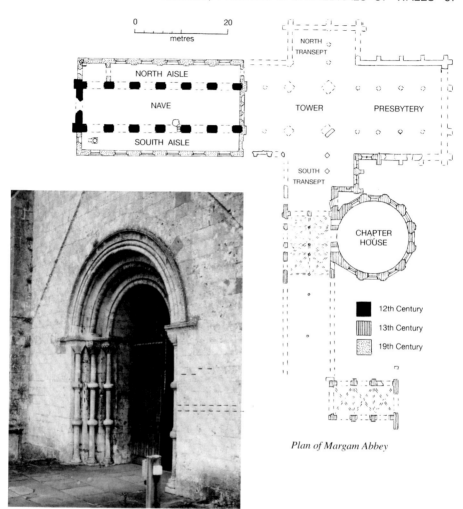

Plan of Margam Abbey

West doorway of Margam Abbey church

Of the mid 13th century eastern parts of the church there remain low walls of the north aisle of the presbytery, parts of the south transept, and a more impressive section of the walls of the south transept east chapels and the presbytery south wall with two-light windows with simple tracery. Part of the vaulted undercroft of the east range also survives. East of it is the chapter-house, a great rarity in being circular inside but twelve sided externally with large lancets set between angled pilaster buttresses. It was begun under Abbot Gilbert, although the rib-vault carried on a circular pillar was probably completed after his death in 1213. The vault survived until the pier collapsed in 1799, to the eternal shame of the Talbot family, who used the room merely as a coal-house. The three vaulted undercroft bays projecting from the east range further south were probably connected with the reredorter. The cloister is thought to have had the unusually large size of about 40m square. No other buildings now remain.

MONKTON PRIORY   *Benedictine*   SM 979015   Just west of Pembroke Castle

In 1093 the death of the local Welsh ruler Rhys ap Tewdor prompted a band of Normans under Roger de Montgomery, Earl of Shrewsbury to push forwards into Wales and establish the castle of Pembroke. The castle soon passed to Roger's son Arnulf who c1098 founded a priory of St Nicholas just across the estuary from the castle as a cell of the abbey of Seez. When alien houses were suppressed in the early 15th century the abbey of Albans took over the role of mother house.

The nave was always parochial and remained in use after the suppression. The chancel fell into ruin and was only made a part of the church again in the restoration of 1879-85, when its south wall was entirely rebuilt. Both parts of the church are long and comparatively narrow, giving an internal length of 50m. The small Norman windows in the nave north wall were blocked when the walls were later thickened internally to carry a plain pointed barrel-vault. The south doorway is 13th century and the porch is 15th century although its outer entrance reuses 13th century keeled shafts with trumpet capitals. The tall, narrow south transeptal tower with anther vault is probably 15th century. A north transept disappeared after the suppression and the blocking wall has against it one of the four massive buttresses later added on the north side. The choir has two 14th century tomb recesses on the north side. A passage leads through to a long chapel close to, but independent of, the choir north wall. A vestry now lies on the site of a vaulted structure which contained a staircase to a west gallery in the chapel.

The church contains two defaced medieval effigies, one of them a priest, and there is an early 16th century canopied tomb, now lacking the brasses on top, Other monuments include those of Sir Francis Meyrick, d1603, Sir John Owen, d1612, and Sir Hugh Owen, d1670. The font of 1882 lies on a 13th century base with eight columns.

Whatever claustral buildings once stood on the north side of the church have now gone. Not far to the NW lies a medieval barn with two high-pointed entrances. Beyond is a circular dovecote and a farmhouse which if medieval may represent a much rebuilt house for the prior. Dramatically perched on a corner 140m SE of the church is the Old Hall, once thought to have been the priory guest house. It has two big upper rooms set over a low undercroft vaulted with heavy ribs, probably 14th century. There is a blind arch on the south end of a shallow wing on the south which contains a porch with a small room off it. The kitchen wing at the east end of the north wall is a later addition.

Monkton Priory Church

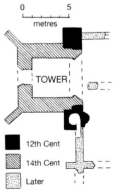

0   5

metres

TOWER

12th Cent

14th Cent

Later

Monmouth: plan of old parts of the priory church

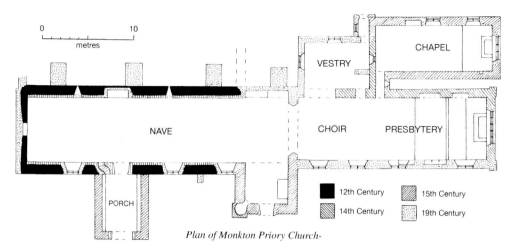

Plan of Monkton Priory Church-

MONMOUTH PRIORY   *Benedictine*   SO 509130   On NE side of the town

William Fitz-Osbern, Earl of Hereford established a castle here before his death in 1071 and by 1075 his son Roger had established the priory church of St Mary not far to the east. All that remains of the medieval church is a diagonally buttressed late 14th century tower squeezed in between two buttress-turrets marking the corners of the Norman nave, which was about 7.5m wide. The southern buttress contains a staircase and has backing onto it the west respond of the original south aisle arcade of round arches on circular piers. Although the choir became ruinous after the priory was suppressed in the 1530s the nave remained in use by the parish. It was demolished in 1732, and then in 1736-37 a new aisled church was built further south so that the tower now opened into the north aisle instead of the nave.

This building was in turn remodelled and given a new east end in 1881-3. The spire on the tower is of c1743, replacing a thicker medieval one. The many 13th and 15th century tiles transferred to the existing south aisle are all that remain of the fittings and monuments of the medieval building. The claustral buildings lay north of the church. Traces of the infirmary were found in 1906 during site clearance for building the Baptist Church in Monk Street. In nearby Priory Street a set of medieval buildings now form a community hall. One projecting wing has a fine late 15th century oriel window over a blocked arch The upper room lighted by this oriel must have been a lodging for the prior or perhaps an estate official or for important guests.

The supposed prior's lodging at Monmouth

NEATH ABBEY   *Cistercian*   SS 738973   1.5km west of the town centre

In October 1130 Abbot Richard and twelve monks came from Savigny in France to set up a new abbey on lands donated by Richard de Granville. He had captured them ten years earlier from the Welsh. The abbey became Cistercian in 1147 along with all the other Savigniac monastic houses. By the 1190s it held extensive estates in Glamorgan, Devon and Somerset. At that time the community considered relocating to Exford in Somerset but this plan was abandoned because of a new abbey being founded at Cleeve just 16km away. As it was there was already competition from the abbey of Margam just 11km further SE along the Glamorgan coast. By the 1290s the Neath community had an annual income of about £236 and was farming an estate of about 5,000 acres. One of their chief holdings was an 800 acre estate at Monknash in the Vale of Glamorgan, where minor ruins and earthworks of the monastic grange still survive.

During the abbacy of Adam of Carmarthen, d1289, the community began building a huge new church. To raise funds for this they handed over large tracts of land to Gilbert de Clare, Earl of Gloucester in return for a fixed annual rent of £100. The church was probably still incomplete when the abbey and its estates suffered from Welsh rebels under Llywelyn Bren. The Owain Glyndŵr rebellion caused similar problems, and in 1423 the abbey was said to be subject to indiscriminate pillaging and that its books, chalices and church ornaments had all been taken. Things improved under Abbot Thomas Franklin, d1441, who was commended by the pope for having restored the buildings, improved services, increased the numbers of monks, and restored the abbey's wealth.

By the end of the 15th century there were only ten monks here and the then abbot built himself a mansion out of some former communal chambers in the east range. The community did, however, enjoy an Indian summer under the Abbot Leyshon Thomas. Despite having an annual income of just £132 in 1535 the abbey survived until Abbot Leyshon and his seven monks surrendered it in February 1539. The buildings and most of the estates were then leased to Thomas Cromwell's nephew Sir Richard Williams. He bought the estate outright for £731 in 1542. It was probably his son Henry who adapted the abbot's house as a mansion, but in the 1590s it was sold to Sir John Herbert. The house was abandoned some time after the middle of the 18th century and the ruins became surrounded by coal mines and iron works. Clearance of the ruins began in 1924 and since 1944 they have been an ancient monument in state care.

The west range at Neath Abbey

Neath: looking across the refectory site to the abbot's house, later an Elizabethan mansion

The late 13th century church at Neath is almost the same size at that at Tintern, with an internal length of 67m, and was once just as magnificent. It is now very fragmentary and has been stripped of all its dressed stonework except for the quoins and gablets high up on the main buttresses of the west front plus a fine stone hand-rail beside the night stair in the south transept. Fallen fragments hint at the former vaults, the bosses of which were adorned with painted shields. Most of the outer walls of the aisles of the seven bay long nave still remain, but little can be said about their windows. The transepts are very ruined and the four bay fully aisled presbytery even more so. The NE crossing pier stands to a fair height but all the other piers are reduced to just bases. Screen walls closed off the western bay of the aisles, and also the two eastern bays and most of the north and south crossing arches, since the monks' choir was located there, with a pulpitum at the west end of it. Each transept had two east chapels and there were four chapels at the east end, one in each aisle and two behind the high altar.

Originally the cloister was about 30m square but it was enlarged to the north after final removal of the much more modest original mid 12th century church, which was aisleless and with just one chapel off each transept. The new church was placed so far north that most of it could be completed whilst the old church (less probably its north transept) remained in use. The western range dates from c1200-20 and is amongst the most complete lay brothers' ranges of any Cistercian monastery in Britain. Some of its original lancet windows still remain. A narrow lane divided it from the west alley of the cloister, a planning feature found in other houses of Savigniac origin, such as Buildwas in Shropshire. A 14th century porch on the west side leads into a vaulted passage. The four bays of the lower storey south of the passage formed the lay brothers' refectory, and their dormitory lay on the upper floor, with triple lancets at the south end and a small latrine at the SW corner. The three bays north of the passage formed cellarage. Beyond is another compartment of two bays later subdivided.

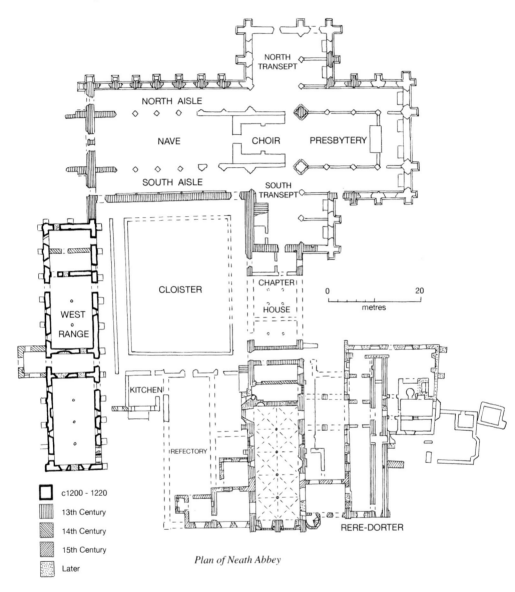

Plan of Neath Abbey

The other ranges around the cloister were all built c1225-50. Only footings remain of the refectory extending southwards from the cloister and of the kitchen west of it, but something can be seen of the lavatorium recesses on either side of the refectory entrance. East of it lay the warming room with the day-stair to the dormitory squeezed into its NE corner. Even less remains of the chapter house in the east range. Between it and the church lay a book room and a sacristy, and south of the chapter house lay a parlour vaulted in two bays by three.

Bridge linking the dormitory and reredorter at Neath

The west range at Neath Abbey

Further south the east range containing the monks' dormitory over rib-vaulted day rooms still stands to full height. Part of it was adapted as a house for the abbot later on and this became the basis of the late 16th century mansion. The day room contains a collection of 14th century tiles from the church and a defaced effigy of what is thought to be Abbot Adam, d1289, holding a model of a church. On the east side of the range a bridge gave access from the dormitory to a long and otherwise detached rere-dorter or latrine. These parts were also incorporated in the Elizabethan house, which had its long gallery extending over the bridge and through the widths of both ranges, whilst kitchens and other service rooms were added beyond the NE corner. South of the bridge and gallery was a light well and than a short range added in the late medieval period between the east range and rere-dorter. The abbot's hall used the former dormitory south end. A wing with the abbot's private rooms extended over the site of the former south end of the refectory. Some way to the NW of the claustral buildings lie ruins of the abbey gatehouse with two large side-arches and a porter's lodge.

Another view of the mansion created from the Abbot's house at Neath

NEWPORT CATHEDRAL   *Secular Canons*   ST 309876   South end of town centre

The parish church of St Woolos on a ridge at the south end of Newport was eventually chosen to be the cathedral of the new diocese of Monmouth created in 1921, the
former priory churches of Abergavenny, Chepstow and Monmouth all being considered
for suitability and rejected. St Woolos was the premier church of the Cantref of Gwyn-
llwg in 1093 when William II granted it to Gloucester Abbey. Evidence of its early importance is demonstrated by the survival of five bays of round-arched arcades on circular
piers with scalloped capitals of c1140 on each side of the nave, with a contemporary
clerestory above. Also Norman, but slightly later, is a fine west doorway of two orders
with figures and birds amongst the foliage on the capitals of the shafts. There are chevrons on the outer arch and a billet-moulded hood. The doorway shows no signs of ever
being external or having been fitted with an actual door. This means that the chapel of
St Mary to the west of it, which is 13th century with restored lancets, must have had an
early predecessor. It contains a font of 1854 on a 12th century shaft and base. There
are also defaced effigies of a cross-legged knight of c1300, an early 14th century lady,
an alabaster late 15th century lady and a torso of a knight, possibly Sir John Morgan
of Tredegar, d1493, whose arms are borne by four weepers on a panel. There is also a
tomb chest of Sir Walter Herbert of St Julian's, d1568, with a very damaged effigy.

West of the chapel lies a tower with a polygonal NE staircase turret and diagonal
buttresses at the other corners. The tower is assumed to have been sponsored by Jasper Tudor, lord of Newport in 1485-95, his headless figure appearing on the south side
together with a shield with a double Tudor rose. The aisles had been widened several
decades earlier and have restored four-light windows and buttresses. The large new
choir of the 1960s, almost as long as the nave, and with its east end soaring above the
sloping ground below, replaced a chancel which was mostly of the 1850 restoration.

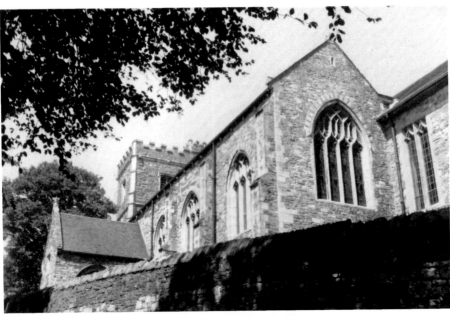

Newport Cathedral from the SE

NEWPORT FRIARY

Augustinian Friars ST 3311188
By the bridge over the Usk

This friary was founded in 1377 by Henry, 2nd Earl of Stafford, who died in 1386 at Rhodes whilst on a pilgrimage to Jerusalem. The friars seem to have taken over an existing chapel of St Nicholas and their first prior Thomas Leche probably came from the Augustinian friary that Henry's father Ralph had founded in the town of Stafford in the 1340s. The friary was damaged by Owain Glyndwr's forces in 1403, but was rebuilt by Henry's grandson Humphrey, who was created Earl of Buckingham in 1444. Jasper Tudor bequeathed the friars here twenty shillings in 1495. The last prior Richard Battle surrendered the house to the royal commissioners in September 1538. An engraving was made of the surviving buildings just before their destruction in 1860. A bus station now lies on the site.

Norman arches at Newport Cathedral

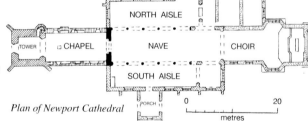

■ 12th Cent ▨ 15th Century

▥ 13th Cent ▦ Later

Plan of Newport Cathedral

NORTH AISLE

TOWER CHAPEL NAVE CHOIR

SOUTH AISLE

PORCH

0   20
metres

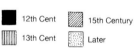

Medieval tile at Monmouth

Newport Friary before it was demolished

PENMON PRIORY   *Augustinian*   SH 630808   In eastern corner of Anglesey

King Einion is said to have founded a monastery at Penmon with his kinsman St Seiriol as its first head. Not far east of the church small drystone structures of great age crowd round a holy well with a fishpond below held in by a dam.

Dating of the various parts of the 12th century cruciform church has been subject to considerable debate. Recent work suggests that the central tower originally stood at the west end of a small nave within the western half of that is now a chancel of 1855 upon mid 13th century foundations, and that the existing nave and transepts at a higher level were added in the mid 12th century. The nave has an original south doorway, a pilaster on each of the north and south sides, and single small round-headed windows facing north, west and south. The south transept has five bays of blind arcading along the inside of its west and south walls. The east wall was rebuilt in 1855, when the north transept was entirely rebuilt. The tower has original small twin round-arched belfry windows facing north and east and is covered with a pyramidal stone roof. Delights within include a 10th or 11th century font, a bearded head and a sheila-na-gig in the south transept, a pillar piscina, and two 10th or 11th century crosses, one showing St Anthony tempted by demons, and the Flight into Egypt, with interlace and knotwork.

In 1237 Llywelyn Fawr granted Penmon to the Celtic monastery 2.5km to the NW on Priestholm (Puffin Island) just across a narrow strait from Penmon and also confusingly dedicated to St Seiriol. On the island a small stone-roofed mid 12th century church tower still survives at SH 651821 adjoining a ruined cottage on the site of a transept, whilst only roof marks remain of a small nave and a 13th century chancel which replaced a tiny vaulted chapel. Nearby are drystone cells against a drystone enclosure wall.

Soon after the grant of 1237 the Celtic community on Priestholm transferred to Penmon and was re-organised as a priory of Augustinian canons. They added a larger new chancel to the church and laid out a cloister 14m square south of it. Continuing the line of the south transept is an inhabited range probably of later medieval date intended as a house for the prior. Rising up from a lower ground level on the south side of the cloister site is a three storey mid 13th century range. It contained a refectory on the second storey at cloister level above an undercroft in the battered base, and a dormitory on the topmost level. The refectory has five square-headed southward facing lancets and a doorway from the cloister, and the dormitory has a tall west lancet. To the east of this range lies an early 16th century block containing a warming house over a kitchen.

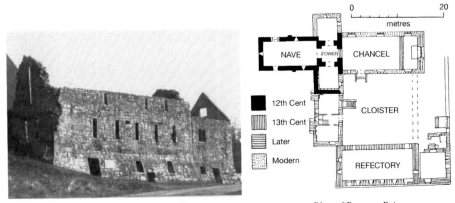

Refectory and dormitory range at Penmon   *Plan of Penmon Priory*

Penmon Priory Church from the SE

Penmon Priory Church from the NW

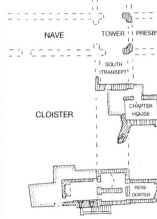

Chapter House at Pill Priory, now a private house   *Plan of Pill Priory*

PILL PRIORY   *Tironensian*   SM 902073   1km north of Milford Haven

In a private garden lies the ivy-clad eastern arch of the 13th century central tower of a small priory founded c1200 by Adam de Roche as a cell of the abbey of St Dogmaels. Old engravings show the tower wall above the surviving arch with two lancets. The south transept end wall remains adjoining a house containing a vault corresponding to the location of a projecting chapter house. Another vault marking the south end of the east range remains further south at the back of the Priory Inn. There was a scandal here in 1403 when Prior Walter Robjoy was accused of keeping a married woman as his mistress and of alienating the priory's possessions, which included a ship. In 1504 the chancel of the church was restored from a ruinous condition. The priory was then said to be free of debt but it was poor enough to be excluded from the clerical subsidies of 1513 and 1517. When suppressed in 1536 the priory had four monks and an annual income of £68 per annum. In 1546 the site was sold to the Barlows of Slebech.

RHUDDLAN FRIARY   *Dominicans*   SJ 029775   4km SE of Rhyl

The farmyard of Abbey Farm represents the cloister of the friary founded c1258 and left isolated when the new Edwardian borough of the 1280s was laid out further NW. In the south range are four blocked square-headed windows facing north towards the yard, and the west range has two blocked 14th century windows facing west. The Buck brothers engraving of 1742 shows more of the original east range surviving that at present. Facing the yard the west range has the upper half of a 14th century cross-slab with four circles and the east range has a defaced effigy in a niche. A fragment of window tracery remains in the farmhouse garden. The late 15th century figure of Christ bound and crucified at Bangor probably came from the vanished church here. Also once located here was the tombstone of William de Freney, Archbishop of Edessa in Syria of 1300 now in the parish church to the north. It was William's uncle Gilbert that had brought the first Dominican friars to England back in the 1230s.

RUTHIN COLLEGE *Augustinian Bonhommes* SJ 124584 In centre of the town

Ruthin originally formed part of the parish of Llanrhudd but a chapel-of-ease was provided by Reginald de Grey, who took over the newly begun castle in 1282. His son John
in 1310 made the chapel into a collegiate church. The college was later occupied by
members of a little-known order, the Augustinian Bonhommes, who had just two other
houses in Britain. They remained until the establishment was suppressed along with the
lesser monasteries in 1536. Their head took the title of Warden also sometimes used
by friars. The title was retained when in 1590 Christ's Hospital was set up for a priest
and twelve poor persons to live in almshouses to the east. The Warden lived in the college buildings, which survive on the west side of a small close on the north side of the
church. They include a five bay undercroft with tierceron vaulting and a pointed tunnel-
vault further north. A north range of c1700 once served the Old Grammar School.

The choir was demolished in 1663, leaving the church as a nave of c1310-20 with
a former central tower at its east end, and a wide south aisle of the 1370s in length
equal to five bays of the nave, plus a sixth bay corresponding to the central tower. The
arcade has octagonal piers and arches with hoodmoulds and headstops. The were no
transepts so the tower never had north and south openings of greater width than wide
doorways which are set in blank arches. The east and west arches have boldly sepa-
rated orders with wave-mouldings and filleted shafts with foliated capitals. The west
window of the aisle could be original work of c1320 reset. Most of the other windows
and the broach spire on the tower are of the 1850s but the roofs are late medieval and
bear arms, badges and inscriptions referring to several families such as the Stanleys.

The headless effigy of a late 14th century
lady is presumably one of the Greys. There
is also part of an effigy of an early 14th century priest. Later monuments include those
of Gabriel Goodman, Dean of Westminster,
d1601, John Parry, d1636, Gabriel Goodman, d1673, and several 18th century monuments of some note. There are also brasses to Dean Goodman's father Edward, 1560,
and mother Ciselye, d1583.

Ruthin College

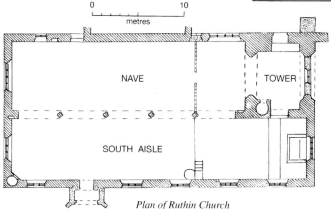

Plan of Ruthin Church

Arcade at Ruthin

ST ASAPH CATHEDRAL   *Secular Canons*   SJ 039743   In middle of the town

St Kentigern (also known as St Mungo) is said to have founded a monastery and episcopal see here c560 after being forced to leave his see at Glasgow, and that when he
returned to Scotland c573 he was succeeded as bishop by St Asaph. The bishopric
eventually fell into abeyance until revived by the Normans in 1143 following similar re-
vivals elsewhere in Wales. The cathedral was burned in 1282 because Bishop Anian II
(whose fine but damaged effigy lies in the north transept) was suspected of supporting
the Welsh rebels. He was only allowed to return after two years of exile and £100 was
then contributed from the royal coffers towards rebuilding the cathedral after a scheme
to move the see to Rhuddlan was abandoned. The cathedral was burned again in 1402,
this time by Owain Glyndwr's Welsh rebel forces.

Building work was underway in 1239, probably on the choir, which retained original
13th century work until the 18th century, but is now essentially the work of Sir Gilbert
Scott in 1867-75, although on the south side the triple lancets of the west bay and the
double lancets of the other two bays reproduce the medieval layout. Originally there
was a two storey chapter house projecting from the middle bay on the north side. In
the choir are a good set of late 15th century stalls with canopies and misericords. They
were moved under the crossing in 1832, only to be replaced back in the choir in 1932.

The nave west wall with gabled and chamfered west buttresses is thought to be 13th
century work but otherwise the aisled nave and the crossing arches and transepts are
all early 14th century. They are characterised by the consistent use of mouldings with
a wave and sunk chamfer. The arcades are of five bays set on quatrefoil shaped piers.
The western bay is shorter than the others and the windows on the south side are out of
syncronicity with the arcades. The aisle doorways and windows have all been restored
and one window on the north has replaced a 15th century doorway east of the present
one. The west doorway of six orders and the six-light window above it with daggers and
mouchettes in the tracery are original, as are the clerestory windows with multifoils set
in squares and the transept windows, with reticulation in the eastern ones. The transept
end windows are of five lights with intersecting ogees and two tier patterns of vesicas
and concave lozenges. The central tower with a NE staircase turret built by Robert Fa-
gan of Chester in 1391-2 has three-light belfry windows with transoms. The upper parts
were rebuilt after storm damage in 1715 and the present parapet is of 1806.

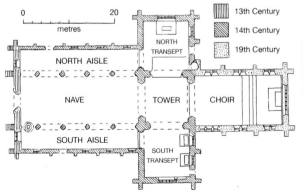

Plan of St Asaph Cathedral   *Misericord seat of choir stall*

The interior of St Asaph Cathedral

St Asaph Cathedral

ST CLEARS *Cluniac* SN281157 East side of old part of the village, south of A40

By the mid 12th century the Norman lord of St Clears had established a small priory and an associated parish church which were affiliated to the Cluniac priory of St Martin-des-Champs near Paris. This link survived until Henry V dissolved the alien priories in 1414. It appears there was sometimes just one monk here and it is unlikely that a regular set of claustral buildings ever existed. The priory must have suffered along with the castle and lordship from frequent Welsh attacks, such as in 1153, 1189, 1215 and 1405. The parish church is quite a substantial building with a massively walled nave 8m wide and 22.5m long. Despite some rebuilding after the roof collapsed in 1680 It is probably mostly 12th century work, but the only certain feature of that period is the chancel arch with two orders of shafts whose bases have been obscured by a raising of the floor. The outer shafts have basket-like capitals. The chancel has one 14th century window on the north side but the walling is probably older. The embattled west tower with a vaulted lowest stage is 16th century. The font may be Norman work recut.

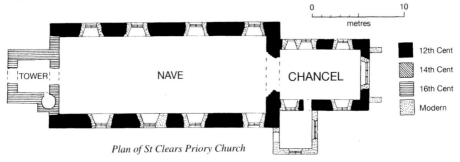

Plan of St Clears Priory Church

The chancel arch at St Clears

Inside the nave of St Davids Cathedral

ST DAVIDS CATHEDRAL *Secular Canons* SM 751253 At west end of the city

In c550 St David, then aged about thirty, arrived from Ireland to found a monastery here, in a location close to the sea, yet sheltered from it. No buildings remain from that period, when monastic life was very harsh, animals not being used or eaten, so that the land had to be tilled by hand and gifts were not accepted, nor was anything individually owned. The Welsh Annals record eleven attacks on the community between 906 and 1089. William of Normandy arrived in 1081 supposedly as a pilgrim, but also to make a political statement. After Rhys ap Tewdwr died in 1093 the Normans took over the monastery and established an episcopal see supported by secular canons. St David was canonised c1120 and it was decreed that two pilgrimages to St Davids were equal to one pilgrimage to Rome, thus ensuring a steady stream of visitors.

Soon after his appointment in 1115, Bernard, first of the Norman bishops, began work on a new cathedral to replace what was probably a motley collection of small and poorly built chapels. He also pleaded for the creation of a separate Welsh arch-diocese led from St Davids but this was firmly resisted by the kings of England and the archbishops of Canterbury. A considerable part of the new cathedral must have stood by 1131, when it was dedicated. Except possibly for some of the thick walling in the transepts, nothing remains of this building. It suffered some sort of disaster in 1182, prompting Bishop Peter de Leia to commence a completely new structure. By the time of his death in 1198 work on the existing nave and aisles of must have been well under way. The nave main body is 10m wide by only 14m high and the piers are remarkably widely spaced, allowing just six bays of round arches adorned with roll-mouldings and chevrons. The piers have alternate circular and octagonal cores to which shafts are attached, triple towards the aisles to allow for vaults that were never built, but singles on the other cardinal points. Most of the capitals are trumpet scallops but there some with foliage and one has tiny human figures. The aisle east ends are unusual, having just doorways instead of true arches through to the transepts.

Higher up the triforium and clerestory are combined and have two bays to each one of the main arcades. The presence of triple shafts makes it likely that vaulting was intended, possibly with cells roofed in either wood or tufa, which is lighter than ordinary stone. The existing ceiling is work of the highest order, unique amongst British cathedrals and probably dating from c1538-9. It is made up of a series of panels, two per bay and six across the width of the nave. After every second panel there are cusped openwork arches, with square pendants set diagonally where they meet. It is quite remarkable that something so ornate was erected here against the wishes of newly appointed Bishop William Barlow, who was keen to transfer the see to Carmarthen. The aisles also have flat 16th century ceilings. During the time of Bishop Henry de Gower they had been heightened and given three light windows but a second attempt to provide vaults seems to have been abandoned at about the time of his death in 1347, which was followed only two years later by the Black Death. On the north side internal flying buttresses were provided c1500 that would not have allowed vaulting.

On the south side is a comparatively modest vaulted porch with an upper room reached by a staircase in the NW corner. It is 14th century but much rebuilt. The west front is almost entirely of the 1880s. Over the years this end of the cathedral has had stability problems, probably not helped by the earthquake of 1247 which is said to have destroyed a "great part" of the building. The east end of the nave has a huge 14th century pulpitum incorporating the tomb of Bishop Gower. In the south aisle is an effigy of priest and a tomb depicting Bishop John Morgan, d1504.

Crossing arches under the tower at St Davids

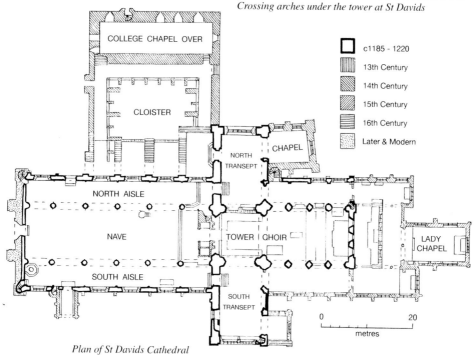

Plan of St Davids Cathedral

The choir stalls at St Davids made when Owen Pole was treasurer, ie 1493-1509 have misericords with oak leaves, an owl, green men, ship-builders, etc. They lie within the crossing arches, three of which had to be rebuilt after the tower collapsed eastwards in 1220. The transepts are quite long and each has three moulded arches of c1210-20 in the east wall. The inner ones lead into the choir aisles and the middle ones were always just blind altar recesses. The outer ones led to chapels. The chapel on the south is about the original size, but is now a 16th and 19th century rebuilding. The northern arch now leads into a larger 14th century vaulted chapel of St Thomas set at an odd angle to the rest of the building. The north transept contains the shrine of St Caradog, d1124, backed against the choir stalls and an effigy of a 14th century priest. The central tower has a 13th century lowest stage, then a taller early 14th century stage with two-light windows, and finally a top stage of c1500 with small belfry windows and an arcaded parapet with eight hexagonal pinnacles.

The choir has four bays but these are much narrower than in the nave. It appears to have been designed in the 1190s to have round arches but has ended up with pointed ones, although the use of chevrons on them suggests they predate the tower collapse of 1220. The east window of three lancets looks like work of the 1190s remodelled at the top in the 1230s. Below is a string course with Greek key ornament and intersecting beaded semicircles. The arcades have alternating circular and octagonal piers with attached shafts. Chevrons appear again on the clerestory windows. There is a clerestory passage on the south side, installed after a plan for ribbed vaulting had ben abandoned. The choir aisles were also intended to have ribbed vaults. The outer wall of the south aisle was rebuilt slightly further out in the late 13th century and both aisles were given three light windows in the 14th century when again springers for vaults were put in at a high level. On the north side of the choir is a shrine of the 1270s made to hold the relics of St David and on the south side is a fine 14th century bishop's throne. In the centre is the Purbeck marble tomb of Edmund Tudor, d1456, father of Henry VII, brought here from the Franciscan friary church at Carmarthen. There are also fine 15th century sedilia. The south aisle of the choir contains a good effigy of Bishop Anselm, d1247, a later 13th century bishop, two 14th century knights and two priests. The north choir aisle has a effigy possibly of Rhys Gryg, d1233. Cromwellian troops took off most of the lead roofs in 1648, leaving the eastern parts of the cathedral to fall into ruin. The transepts were re-roofed in 1696 but the choir long lay ruinous.

Monuments of bishops in St Davids Cathedral

Looking down onto the east end of St Davids Cathedral

Until the Trinity Chapel was created to fill the space in the 16th century there was an open gap (unparalleled in any other cathedral) between the east lancets of the choir and the passage linking extensions of the aisles to give access to the Lady Chapel. Oddly out of line to the south of the main exis of the cathedral, and left roofless from 1775 until the 1890s, the Lady Chapel appears to be 13th century but mostly rebuilt c1500, with sedilia of that period. No surviving features support the claim it was built by Bishop Martin in the early 14th century. A blocked original lancet remains on the south side. Outside in the passage is an effigy perhaps of Archdeacon John de Fakenham, d1274. In the retrochoir south aisle are effigies of a cross-legged knight, another knight and a priest all of the 14th century, and of Archdeacon John Hiot, d1419. Several fragments of 13th century cross-slabs are reset in the altar of the Trinity Chapel.

The cloister about 22m square on the north side of the cathedral and the chapel raised over a vaulted undercroft on the north side of it formed part of the college of St Mary founded by Bishop Houghton in 1365. Huge 16th century buttresses intrude into the southern part of the cloister. It appears that there was an upper room over the western alley of the cloister. From this alley a wide set of steps led up under a belfry turret to the chapel, which was restored from ruin in the 1960s for use as a general hall. Ruins of the lodgings of the college fellows remain to the NE.

Some way west of the cathedral is the ruined bishops' palace. Much of it, with fine arcaded parapets, was the work of Henry Gower, d1347. North of the palace lay the houses of the archdeacons of Brecon, Cardigan and St Davids. After the cathedral central tower fell in 1220 an octagonal belfry was built high up to the SE. Adjoining it is the 14th century gateway into the close from the city. The close wall, now ruinous, surrounded all the clergy houses and once had three other gateways.

ST DOGMAEL'S ABBEY *Tironensian* SN 164458 1.5km west of Cardigan

In 1113 Robert Fitz-Martin brought back a prior and twelve monks from Tiron in France to found a priory within his lordship of Cemaes. The monks are assumed to have taken over premises formerly occupied as a Celtic monastery. In 1118 their numbers were doubled by a fresh intake of new monks from Tiron and the community was upgraded from a priory to an abbey. The abbot of St Dogmaels was required to visit Tiron every three years to maintain strong links with the mother-house. Times were hard for the new abbey. Its Norman patron was defeated and forced to retreat southwards in 1136, and in 1138 the abbey was raided by Vikings. In 1188 Gerald of Wales stayed a night here with Archbishop Baldwin of Canterbury on their tour of Wales in support of the Third Crusade. Ten years later Gerald and Abbot Walter of St Dogmaels were rivals for the vacant see of St Davids. According to Gerald, Abbot Walter could neither read nor write. In the end the pope quashed the election and neither of them got the post.

Better English control of the area, in conjunction with the rebuilding of the royal castle at Cardigan in stone, brought better times for the abbey in the 1230s when the claustral buildings were finally completed. In 1296 the abbot petitioned Edward I that the abbey was "much ruined and impoverished by the war that has been in their country" and again in 1318 it was claimed that the abbey was unable to pay its taxes. Numbers were reduced by the plague in 1349, and when the bishop of St Davids made a visitation in 1402 there was just an abbot and three other monks, and licentiousness was said to be rife. Another visitation in 1504 found a better state of affairs, with the chancel of the church recently repaired and six monks under an abbot. When suppressed in 1536 the abbey had an abbot and eight monks and an annual income of £87. The lands went to the Bradshaws of Presteign who built a mansion on the site. The central part of the nave of the abbey church was used as a parish church from c1640 until c1710, when a new church to the north to erected on the site now occupied by a church of 1847. The abbey ruins have been in state guardianship since 1934.

North transept of St Dogmaels Abbey

South side of cloister looking east

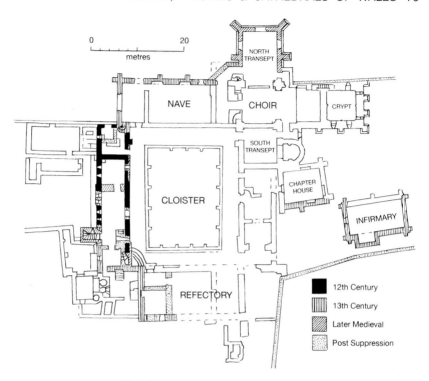

Plan of St Dogmaels Abbey

As laid out in the mid 12th century the abbey church was designed with a short presbytery with an apse east of a crossing over the choir stalls, transepts each with a single eastern apse, and an aisled nave. Of this there remain parts of the crossing piers and footings of the south transept with its apse which survived all the later alterations. In the 13th century the presbytery was lengthened up to a new square end over a vaulted crypt. The nave was finally completed without aisles except for just one bay on the north side. The space originally designated for the south aisle became part of an enlarged cloister. In the 14th century the nave east end was filled with a pulpitum. The north transept was rebuilt in a longer form c1500 with diagonal buttresses and without a chapel opening off it. This part still stands to eaves level.

Only footings remain of the cloister and the south and east ranges around it, including a refectory on the south side. In the late 13th or early 14th century a new angle-buttressed chapter house set at a slight angle to the other buildings was built beyond the east range. To the SE of it lies in infirmary of which the west, south and east walls still stand high with remains of vaulting and angle buttresses. Low walls remain of the west range which was given a staircase turret on the west side in the late medieval period, and a large new wing to accommodate guests was added onto the west side of the north end. The Bradshaws' mansion probably incorporated these parts, and the numerous rooms including some with ovens by the SW corner are certainly of the post-suppression period.

SLEBECH COMMANDERY   *Knights Hospitallers*   SN 032139   8km W of Narberth

Founded in 1161, Slebech was the only preceptory of the Knights Hospitallers in Wales to function as such all through the medieval period. It was the centre for all their operations in the diocese of St Davids. A preceptory at Garway in Herefordshire served the rest of mid and south Wales, and operations in North Wales originally centred at Ysbity Ifan were later transferred to a preceptory at Halston in Shropshire. Slebech Hall of the 1770s stands on the site of the domestic buildings, which became a mansion of the Barlow family after the preceptory was suppressed in 1540.

The medieval church beside the hall was unroofed in 1844 after a new church (now itself closed) was built to the NW. The thin chancel arch dates the nave to the 14th century. The chancel itself, probably 15th century, is comparatively long and has a tomb recess on the south side. The east window has lost its tracery and the side windows have later brick tops. Transeptal chapels were added on either side of the nave in the early 16th century. That on the north has three-light windows and adjoins a tall porch-tower of the same period. The other transept was rebuilt in the 18th century. From this church have come the alabaster effigies thought to be of Sir Henry Wogan of Picton, d1475, and his wife, now in the county museum at Haverfordwest.

The ruined church at Slebech

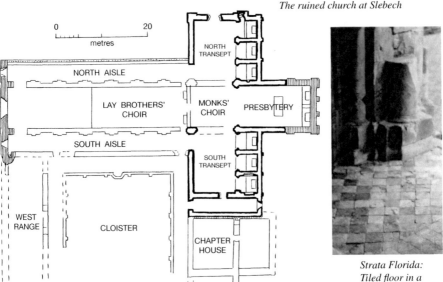

Plan of Strata Florida Abbey

Strata Florida: Tiled floor in a south chapel

STRATA FLORIDA ABBEY   *Cistercian*   SN 746658   11km S of Devil's Bridge

Robert Fitz-Stephen appears to have founded this abbey in 1164. In the autumn of that year the Welsh under Rhys ap Gruffudd began to drive the Normans out of Ceredigion. Within two years they captured both Fitz-Stephen and his principal stronghold of Cardigan. Benedictine monks probably would have been driven out with the fleeing Normans but Cistercians were more acceptable to the Lord Rhys. A charter of 1184 records him as patron of the building works then in progress and it became a centre of Welsh culture and influence, being the burial place of the noted poet Dafydd ap Gwilym. In and around the chapter house were buried members of the Dinefwr branch of the descendants of the Lord Rhys. At the abbey parts of the annals known as the Brut y Tywysogion are thought to have been recorded. In 1238 all the Welsh princes and nobles were summoned by Llywelyn Fawr of Gwynedd to the abbey to swear allegiance to his son Dafydd. For a time during the Glyndwr revolt in the early 15th century the abbey was deserted by the monks and in military occupation. The abbey had an annual income of £118 when it was suppressed in 1536 and the property passed to the Stedman family, later going to the Powells of Nantoes. Part of the site was handed over to the Church of Wales and in 1931 was transferred to the state as an ancient monument.

   The ruins lie on the south bank of the Teifi and comprise low walls of the church, chapter house and cloister. A farmhouse stands on the site of the refectory and the former outer court beyond the very fragmentary western range is now a garden. The church had a short presbytery and transepts each with three chapels of c1180-1210. A seven bay nave was added c1210-25, whilst the presbytery gained a high vault and an extra eastern bay with clasping corner buttresses c1250, bringing the internal length to 65m. In the 15th century the high altar was moved further west again to allow room behind it for two chapels. These and the transept chapels retain their altar bases.

   The monks' stalls lay under the crossing, not further west, as was usual. Another unusual feature was the placing of the nave piers upon walls 1.5m high only broken by gaps in the westernmost bay. This end has the finest feature of the ruin, a sumptuous round arched central west doorway with five continuous rolls connected by bands with spiral ends. The south aisle window also survives. The many tiles remaining in the chapels appear to have been part of a refurbishment after the church was set on fire by lightning in 1285. The crossing arches appear rather slender for a tower so it is uncertain where the great bell consecrated by the Bishop of Banger in 1254 was set up. It had been purchased for the great sum of 97 marks and two cows.

To the south is the northern half of a cloister 30m square with late medieval inner walls divided into five bays on each side, each once having a window of five round-headed lights. The chapter house originally projected beyond the east range but in the 14th century was reduced to about half its former size.

The great west doorway at Strata Florida Abbey

STRATA MARCELLA ABBEY   *Cistercians*   SJ 251104   4km NE of Welshpool

A memorial stone set up by the A483 in 1970 is the only reminder of an abbey founded in 1170 by Owain Cyfeiliog with monks sent over from Whitland. In 1201 it in turn sent out monks to found the abbey of Valle Crucis. By 1328 there were only eight monks left here and four years later the local English lord John de Charlton had them evicted for laxity (and perhaps because they were Welsh). They were replaced by English monks from Buildwas. In the 16th century the community got into debt. Their lands were already in the hands of Lord Powis when their house was suppressed in 1536. Three bells were taken off to Chirk and an organ went to St Mary's Church at Shrewsbury.

Talley Abbey

Excavations in the 1890s found footings of parts of a church 80m long with a typical Cistercian short presbytery of the late 12th century and a 60m long aisled nave with piers of 13th century type with clustered shafts. There appears to have been a central tower, perhaps as a result of some remodelling in the 14th century. A few tiles and carved stones were taken off to the Powysland Museum in Welshpool. Probably from the abbey are a fireplace at Trewern House, a good stiff-leaf capital made into a font at Buttington, and possibly the fine 13th century doorway at Llanfair Caereinion church.

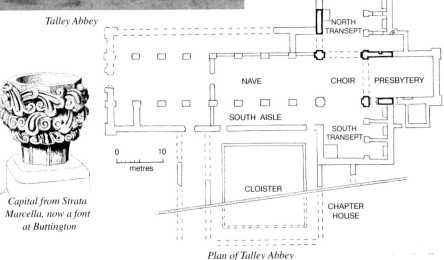

Capital from Strata Marcella, now a font at Buttington

Plan of Talley Abbey

TALLEY ABBEY   *Premonstratensians*   SN 633229   10km north of Llandeilo

Rhys ap Gruffudd founded this abbey dedicated to St Mary and St John the Baptist probably in the 1180s. He was then at peace with King Henry II, whose justiciar Ranulf Glanville (then ruling the Welsh marches) particularly favoured the white canons of the order of Premontre, being directly or indirectly involved in the founding of six of their houses in England at that time. The canons at Whitland first had to contend with hostility from the Cistercians at Whitland, the matter being taken first to Canterbury and then to Rome before being decided in Talley's favour. After Rhys died in 1197 his family fought over his inheritance, which was eventually split into two lines, one based at Dinefwr and the other at Dryslwyn. Both branches continued to be patrons of the abbey but this was not sufficient for completion of the church to its originally intended great size.

The abbey was impoverished as a result of the Edward I's campaigns against the princes of South Wales in 1277 and had to be taken into the king's hands in the following year. The king distrusted the Welsh canons at Talley and maintained they were living immorally. In 1284 the general chapter of the order sent down a new English abbot to improve things at Talley, which in future was to be monitored by the abbey of Welbeck. Conditions at Talley were still causing concern for the general chapter in 1291, resulting in the abbots of Newhouse and Halesowen being sent to make reforms. During the 14th century Talley became recognised as a daughter house of Halesown. Neglect by two successive abbots resulted in the abbey being again placed under royal protection in 1381. The Glyndwr revolt and a serious of law-suits added to the community's misfortunes. When suppressed in 1536 the abbey had eight canons and annual revenues of £136. The presbytery and tower remained in use as a parish church until a new church was built further north in 1772. The ruins have been in state care since 1933.

Standing remains of the abbey comprise the plain pointed north and east crossing arches and two walls of the tower above them to a height of 26m, plus most of the west wall of the north transept. Low walls remain of the rest of the church and the northern half of a cloister 23m square together with slight remains of parts of the east and west ranges. A farmhouse lies on the side of the south range. The church was laid out on a generous scale with an intended internal length of 70m (longer than the cathedral of St Davids at that time), allowing for a fully aised nave eight bays long, a presbytery of three bays with turrets clasping the eastern angles, transepts each with three chapels, and a sacristy on the south side beyond the innermost chapel. A wall joining the western pier to the aisle wall suggests that small western towers may have been intended. In the end only one bay at the east end of the north aisle was ever built, and the four western bays of the nave and south aisle were abandoned after the lower parts of the walls and piers had been built. A crosswall was inserted between the fourth set of rectangular piers from the central tower. The NE crossing pier is moulded but the two surviving tower arches are quite plain. All the chapels retain their altar bases. The innermost chapel on the north side was later slightly extended and the walls between the chapels were then pierced.

Innermost north transept chapel at Talley

TINTERN ABBEY   *Cistercian*   SO 533001   By River Wye, 6km north of Chepstow

Tintern was second Cistercian house established in the British Isles, being founded in 1131 for monks from L'Aumone in France under patronage from Walter Fitz-Richard, lord of nearby Chepstow and also of Clare in Suffolk. Walter was related by marriage to Bishop William of Winchester who had founded the earliest Cistercian house in Britain at Waverley in Surrey. By 1139 the community at Tintern was large enough to send out monks to found a daughter house at Kingswood in Gloucestershire. During the period 1148 -57 the community was ruled by the energetic Abbot Henry, a reformed former robber, who during his abbacy visited both the Pope and the Cistercian spiritual leader St Bernard. A second daughter house known as Tintern Parva was founded on the Irish estates of William Marshal in Co Wexford in 1203. Later lords of Chepstow such as William Marshal II in the 1220s and Roger Bigod in the 1290s made generous land grants to Tintern abbey which enabled the original 12th century buildings to be gradu-ally replaced on a larger scale. By that time the abbey was farming 3000 acres in the Welsh valleys and had a flock of over 3200 sheep. Roger Bigod's gift of the Norfolk manor of Acle later provided a quarter of the community's income.

Tintern was the wealthiest abbey in Wales with an annual income of £192 when it was surrendered to the Crown in September 1536 by Abbot Wyche, who was gener-ously pensioned off. Most of the estates went to the then lord of Chepstow, Henry Somerset, 2nd Earl of Worcester, by whom the buildings were stripped of their lead roofs. Before long the district was full of industrial premises making iron, brass and wire, and workers' tenements were created within the ruined abbey. In the mid 18th century the Wye Valley became popular with "Romantic" upper class tourists and the ruined church began to be valued for its scenic qualities. The site was purchased by the Crown from the Duke of Beaufort in 1901 and became a state-run ancient monu-ment in 1914, since when the ruins have been cleared of later encroachments and much consolidation carried out, including the rebuilding of the south arcade of the nave with steel beams being inserted within the piers and the aisle roof.

Tintern Abbey from the south-east

Most of the magnificent new church begun in 1269 still exists, although the north arcade of the six bay long nave has gone and the south aisle is the only part still covered by a roof. Masses began to be held within the aisled four bay long east end in 1288 by which time the building was mostly complete as far west as the second bay of the nave. Work resumed after a slight pause and the church was consecrated in 1301. Construction of the western and upper parts continued into the 1320s, when a huge pulpitum was installed in the eastern part of the nave. The new church measuring 69m long internally was positioned so that most of the original aisle-less 12th century church 50m long could remain in use whilst the eastern parts were constructed, only the south transept and its two chapels of the older building initially needing to be removed to make way for the crossing arches of the new building set over the monks' choir. Finally, after the old church was removed (its position is now

Arcades in the church at Tintern Abbey

marked out on the ground), the northern parts of the new church were built and the cloister was extended southwards to meet up with the outer wall of the north aisle of the nave, in the east end of which is a finely moulded doorway of c1300.

The church has regular buttressing and two-light windows in the aisles and the west wall of the south transept. The pairs of chapels east of the transepts have three-light windows. In the north transept there survives the night staircase up to the dormitory. In the clerestory the windows are also of two lights and the buttresses are pilasters. Originally the nave and presbytery must have had parapets at the top, set on corbelling which still remains. There was never a central tower and the triforium is no more than a plain band with an undercut roll below and above it. The presbytery arcades have quatrefoil-shaped piers, originally with four additional detached shafts, and set on lozenge-shaped bases. In the nave the additional shafts are integral and the piers were built up from screen walls framing the monks choir and the lay brothers' choir.

The elaborately moulded east window in the presbytery is an enormous opening originally of eight lights, although only the thick central mullion has survived. What little remains of the tracery shows it was of Geometrical type with three great circles enclosing patterns of cinquefoils, four of them in the top circle and three in the others. The south transept has a SW staircase turret and a doorway set into the lower part of a huge window, once of six lights. The main west window is better preserved and has seven lights grouped into a pattern of two-three-two. The mullions there have shaft rings and the window frame is also shafted and elaborately moulded, all part of a composition aimed at impressing visitors arriving from this direction. There are four main arches within the tracery, the middle ones overlapping, and within them are pointed trefoils under lobed daggers. Above this window was another of five lights and below are twin doorways under blind arcading within the head of one moulded master-arch.

The NE corner of the main cloister at Tintern Abbey

The layout of claustral buildings to the north of the church at Tintern is the most extensive now surviving in Wales. Most of them are 13th century but 12th century walling remains in the chapter house south wall, the west wall of the cloister and on either side of the southern half of the day rooms under the dormitory. Parts standing above the lower walls include the parlour and its still-roofed west porch with upper rooms probably for the cellarer on the west side of the cloister, part of the lay brothers' NW range once containing a dormitory set over a refectory to the north of the storeroom beside the parlour, plus most of the north side of the cloister with parts of the main refectory. This splendid room is set from south to north and has a stair up to a former pulpit in its west wall. Part of the east wall still has pairs of two-light windows with plate-tracery in each bay above a plain dado. The recesses on either side of the once finely moulded refectory doorway formed the lavatorium or hand-washing place.

West of the refectory lies the very ruinous kitchen (now lacking its central fireplace) and to the east of the refectory is the warming house, with its south end still vaulted. The day rooms were of six bays by two with a central row of piers to support vaulting. West of them lies the day stair and east of them lies the base of the reredorter flushed by a drain firstly running under the western range, kitchen and refectory and then heading out east under the infirmary kitchen. The chapter house is very ruined but enough survives to show it was vaulted in five bays by three supported on two rows of slender piers and that the entrance was in the form of a triple-arched arcade. The western bays were probably just a vestibule before the chapter house itself in the heavily buttressed two east bays, where there is a wall bench. South of here lay a library and sacristy set end to end. Little remains of the cloister alleys, which were rebuilt in the 1470s.

The day rooms, chapter house and reredorter enclosed the eastern half of a second cloister extending out to the infirmary, which is now reduced to footings. A diagonally set corridor also connected the infirmary hall with the north aisle of the presbytery. The infirmary consisted of a central hall 32m long by 7m wide flanked by aisles later converted into a series of smaller rooms with fireplaces. Beyond the infirmary kitchen to the north lie the footings of the abbot's house composed of a 13th century chamber block extending east from a large 14th century block containing a hall over several rooms. Parts of the precinct walls remain with a main gate and gate-chapel (now part of a house), a water-gate, and also footings of guest apartments.

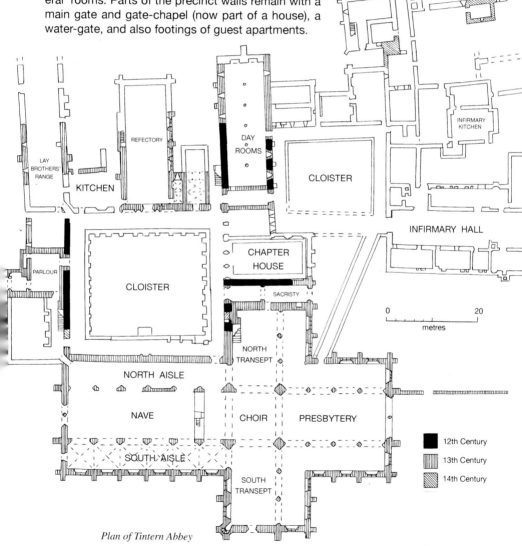

Plan of Tintern Abbey

USK PRIORY   *Benedictine Nuns*   SO 379008   At sourth end of the town

The nunnery here seems to have been founded in the short interval between 1174, when the de Clares recovered Usk from Welsh control, and the death of Richard "Strongbow" de Clare in 1176. Of the church of that period there remains only the central tower on arches of two orders with triplets of semi-circular shafts, plus part of the north transept west wall surviving at the east end of the aisle and the chamfered-cornered font with four shafts set around the stem. A 19th century vestry occupies the site of the north transept. Both transepts and the vaulted presbytery were destroyed after the nunnery was suppressed in 1535. The tower has pairs of simple round-arched belfry lights, a corbelled parapet and a circular NW staircase turret.

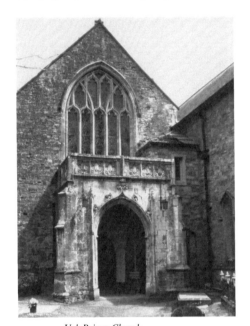

Usk Priory Church

The parochial nave was given a north aisle with an arcade of wide double-chamfered arches on circular piers in the mid 13th century. About two hundred years later, probably at the expense of Sir William Herbert, the aisle was doubled in width and given lierne-vaulted two storey porches facing west and north. The four-light windows have been restored. The west bay of the nave is an addition of 1844, when the south wall was also rebuilt and a vault inserted over the crossing to fit it up as a sanctuary. The eastern bay of the nave and aisle are divided off by a 15th century screen of a West Country type. Fixed on the screen is a very rare brass plate with an inscription to Adam of Usk, d1430, a chronicler and benefactor. The only other medieval monument is a worn effigy of a man in 14th century civilian dress lying in the churchyard.

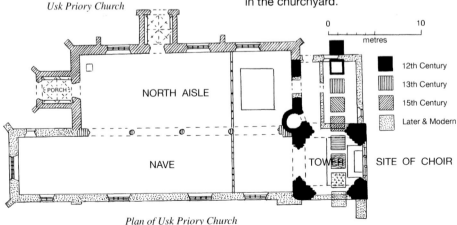

■	12th Century
▥	13th Century
▨	15th Century
░	Later & Modern

Plan of Usk Priory Church

Part of a wooden frieze remains in the large house of 1868 south of Usk parish church. Another part of the frieze surviving in the manor house of Cefntilla in the parish of Llandenny has shields with heraldry and emblems of the Passion in foliate scrolls and the initials of Ellen Williams, prioress of Usk Priory when it was suppressed in 1535. Of about the same period is the two storey gatehouse by the churchyard entrance. It has square-headed windows and a west fireplace in the upper room.

The tower of Usk Priory

Valle Crucis Abbey from the SW

VALE CRUCIS ABBEY   *Cistercian*   SJ 205442   2km NW of Llangollen

In January 1201 monks arrived here from Strata Marcella to colonise a new abbey founded by Madog ap Gruffydd Maelor, who was buried within it in 1236. The abbey was named after the 9th century cross of Eliseg lying just to the NW on an earlier tumulus. Work on the church was interrupted by a fire in the mid 13th century, after which the east end was completed rather higher than originally intended. It is uncertain whether the vaulting of the presbytery allowed for in the original design was ever completed. The upper part of the nave west gable has an inscription referring to Adam, whose abbacy occupied the middle years of the 14th century. The chapter house and east range are late 14th century in style but may actually be of the 1420s, following possible damage inflicted during the rebellion of Owain Glyndwr. Late in the 15th century Abbot David created a new lodging for himself by dividing off the northern end of the dormitory, which was then provided with a fireplace and an external timber staircase up from the cloister, and a private room created over the sacristy. It is possible that by that time only the eastern parts of the church remained in use, walled off from the empty nave. After the abbey was suppressed in 1536 it passed to Sir William Pickering, whose heiress married into the Wootton family. The east range remained in use as a house until at least the 1650s but was ruinous during the 18th century. It was re-roofed as a farmhouse c1800 and is still roofed now. Archaeological investigation of the site began as early as the 1840s and led to subsequent clearance and conservation of the remains. The ruins have been in state care since 1950.

West doorway capitals at Valle Crucis

The west gable at Valle Crucis

The church has a presbytery of two bays east of a crossing with transepts each with two eastern chapels. All the buttressing is in the form of shallow pilasters, typical of an early 13th century date. Originally the monks' choir lay in the eastern part of the aisled nave of five bays but it was later moved eastwards under the crossing. The pulpitum closing the west arch of the crossing is later medieval but incorporates 13th century parts from an older pulpitum further west. When the SW crossing pier was rebuilt after the fire a solid wall replaced the arcade arch west of it. The nave arcades are reduced to just pier bases and the north aisle wall only survives to dado level. The main west gable stands complete with a wheel-window over a triple set of two-light windows with sexfoils on each side and an octofoil in the middle. Below them is a grand central doorway of four orders. There is also a doorway in the north aisle west wall. The south transept stands to full height and the chapels there still retain their vaults, the southern one having sedilia and a piscina. Later on a heightening of the roofs allowed the insertion of a chamber over these chapels. The presbytery also stands nearly complete and has three east lancets with the eastern one slightly taller. The pilasters between these windows widen out high up to externally frame an upper row of two more acutely pointed lancets, a most unusual piece of mid 13th century design after the fire. There are tomb recesses on either side of the western bay of the presbytery, although the southern one is mostly a modern reconstruction.

South of the church lay a cloister about 25m square. Only footings remain of the west range and the kitchen at the SW corner and just low walls of a refectory extending southwards from the south side, with a pulpit staircase on the west side. The east range is modest in size compared with the church. Next to the church a vaulted sacristy extends the width of both the adjoining transept and the chapels. Next comes the square chapter house vaulted in three bays by three with four wave-moulded central piers without capitals. There are three-light east windows with reticulated tracery and a row of blank recesses on the south side. A vaulted passage leading out to the cemetery lies between the chapter house and the lower part of the rere-dorter at the south end of the dormitory. Reset in the east end of the passage is a 13th century doorway.

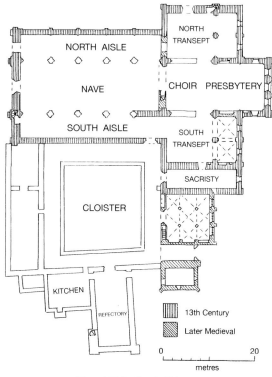

Plan of Valle Crucis Abbey

The dormitory is still roofed and has six west lancets, one for each of the monks' cubicles. The doorway and four-light window on the west side and the fireplace on the east side mark the northern part later divided off to create the abbot's hall, with its chamber further east over the sacristy. One of these rooms once had a fine fretted ceiling mentioned by the contemporary poet Gutun Owain. The dormitory now contains a fine set of twenty grave slabs removed from the church. One may be that of the founder and another particularly fine example is that of his great-grandson Madog ap Gruffydd, d1306. A rare dated graveslab of 1290 is to Gweirca ferch Owain. There is also an early 14th century half effigy of Ieuaf ab Adda.

Valle Crucis Abbey from the SE

WHITLAND ABBEY   *Cistercian*   SN 209181   2km NNE of Whitland

In a field lie footings of a church with a fully aisled eight bay long nave and a crossing with transepts each with two each chapels and a presbytery no longer than either of the transepts, i.e. just of two bays. The arcade piers were rectangles like those of Margam. Footings also remain of the west range of the claustral buildings, with scars of two vaults. Beyond here one higher fragment of an outlying building still stands high. Further up the valley are traces of fishponds and millponds with associated leats.

The church was probably begun in the 1150s with patronage from the Lord Rhys. Whitland was thus the earliest of the Cistercian houses in the Welsh parts of Wales and eventually had seven daughter houses in Wales and two in Ireland. The abbey was raided by a band of Norman knights in 1257 and was damaged by English forces mustered there either in 1277 or 1282. The estates were valued at £43 annually in 1291 and declined still further later on, the situation not being helped by the abbot taking the side of Owain Glyndwr's rebels in the early 15th century. In later years there were never more than eight monks and sometimes only five. In the 1580s Dr John Vaughan had a fine manor house on part of the site with twenty-two rooms and windows of up to ten lights. Iron was worked on the site from the mid 17th century, making use of the abbey's watercourses. This finally ceased in 1810 and the walled garden on the site of the cloister was laid out in the 1840s, when the Morgan heiress and her husband built a new house to the SE. The site was excavated in the 1920s and again in the 1990s.

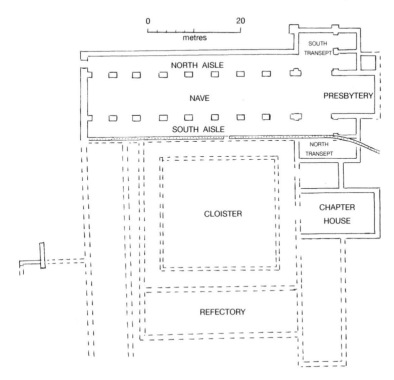

Plan of Whitland Abbey

The last traces of Whitland Abbey

YSBYTY IFAN   *Knights Hospitaller*   SH 843487   13km SSE of Llanrwst

The Knights Hospitallers were established here c1190, and were given more endowments in the 1220s by Llywelyn Fawr. In 1294 its functions as a commandery were united with that of Halston in Shropshire, although it continued to function as a hospice in the 14th century. After the Hospitallers were suppressed in 1540 the church became parochial. The existing building is of 1860 but contains three 14th century monumental slabs and damaged early 16th century effigies of Rhys Fawr ap Meredydd, standard bearer to Henry Tudor at Bosworth in 1485, and his wife and their son Robert ap Rhys, chaplain to Cardinal Wolsey.

OTHER MEDIEVAL RELIGIOUS HOUSES IN WALES

BURRY HOLMS SS 403926 Hermitage of St Kenydd-atte-Holme mentioned 1195.
  Site on tidal island by the Gower excavated in 1960s. Parts of a chapel were found.
CARNO SN 963965 Moated site of a grange of the Knights Hospitallers near parish
  church of St John, of 1867, but with possible medieval work on the north site.
EGRYN SH 595202 Late 15th century farmhouse north of Barmouth now held by
  National Trust. Site of a hospital of St Mary with a chapel in the 14th century.
LLANBADARN FAWR SN 599810 Large early 13th century church on site of Celtic
  monastery. Monks from Gloucester installed c1116, driven out by the Welsh c1135.
RHAYADER The Dominicans had some presence here, probably not a friary as such,
  perhaps a lodging to house a visiting friar or two sent up from the friary at Brecon.
The Knights Templar appear to have had hospitals at Rhuddlan and Templeton near Narberth. The Llanwddyn Hospitium at SH 998194 was only a farm or grange and has now vanished.

FURTHER READING

Buildings of Wales vols for: Cardigan & Carmarthen (2006), Clwyd (1986), Glamorgan
  (1995), Gwent (2000), Gwynedd (2009), Pembrokeshire (2004), Powys (1979).
R.C.A.H.M.W inventories of ancient monuments: Anglesey, Caernarfon, Carmarthen,
  Denbighshire, Flintshire, Merioneth, Pembroke, Radnorshire.
The Cistercians in Wales, David M. Robinson, 2006
The Monastic Orders in South Wales 1066 - 1349, F.G. Cowley, 1977
The Welsh Church from Conquest to Reformation, Glanmor Williams, 1976.
Periodicals: Archaeologia Cambrensis, Medieval Archeology

GLOSSARY OF TERMS

Aisle	- A passage beside part of a church.
Apse	- A semi-circular chapel or a similarly shaped east end of a church.
Ashlar	- Masonry of large blocks cut to even faces and square edges.
Aumbry	- A recess for storing books or vessels.
Bays	- Divisions of an elevation defined by regular vertical features.
Chancel	- The eastern member of a church reserved for priests and choristers.
Chapter House	- A room where monks, priests or friars met daily to conduct business.
Chevrons	- Vs usually arranged in a continuous sequence to form a zigzag.
Choir	- A part of a monastic church containing stalls for monks, nuns or friars.
Claustral	- To do with or belonging to a cloister.
Clerestory	- An upper storey pierced by windows lighting the floor below.
Cloister Alley	- A walkway along one side of a cloister.
Cloister Garth	- The central court or garden of a cloister, surrounded by four alleys.
Corbel	- A projecting or overhanging stone bracket.
Cruciform Church	- Cross-shaped church with transepts forming the arms of the cross.
Cusps	- Projecting points between the foils of a foiled Gothic arch.
Dado	- Lower part of a wall, or its decorative treatment.
Dog-tooth	- Four cornered stars placed diagonally and raised pyramidally.
Fleuron	- Decorative carved shape like a flower or leaf.
Hood-moulding	- A narrow band of stone projecting out over a window or doorway.
Jamb	- The side of a window, doorway or other opening.
Lancet	- A long and comparatively narrow window, usually pointed headed.
Lavatorium	- A lavatory or washing place, usually next to the refectory entrance.
Mendicant	- Begging, or living solely on alms.
Merlons	- The upstanding parts of a crenellated parapet on a wall or tower.
Nave	- The part of a church in which the lay congregation stood or sat.
Ogival Arch	- Topped by a curve which is partly convex and partly concave.
Oratory	- Small chapel either standing alone or forming part of a large building.
Oriel	- A bay window projecting on corbelling.
Piscina	- A stone basin used for rinsing out holy vessels after a mass.
Presbytery	- The part of a monastic church containing the high altar.
Prior	- The head person of a priory or friary or the deputy head of an abbey.
Pulpitum	- Stone screen shutting off a choir, forming a backing for choir stalls
Quoin	- A cut stone used to form part of a corner.
Refectory	- The main dining room of a monastic house.
Reredorter	- The toilet of a monastic house, usually at the far end of a dormitory.
Respond	- Half pier bonded into a wall and carrying one end of an arch.
Reticulation	- Window tracery with a net-like appearance.
Rood Screen	- A screen with a crucifix mounted on it between a nave and a chancel.
Sacristy	- A part of a church where vestments and sacred vessels were kept.
Sedilia	- Seats for clergy (usually three in the south wall of a chancel or choir.
Spandrel	- The surface between two arches or between an arch and a corner.
Transept	- A cross-arm projecting at right-angles from the main body of a church.
Transom	- A horizontal member dividing upper and lower lights in a window.
Triforium	- Middle storey of a church, either a blind arcade or an arcaded passage.
Vesica	- A pointed oval or eye-shaped opening.
Walking Place	- A cross passage between the nave and the choir of a friary church.
Warming House	- The only room in a monastery with a fireplace (apart from the kitchen).